T0083533

Cornerstone

The Birth of the City in Mesopotamia

Pedro Azara

Translated by Jeffrey Swartz

TENOV BOOKS

First published in Spanish as *Piedra Angular*
© Editorial Tenov December 2012

Revised English edition published in September 2015

© of the text: Pedro Azara
© of the translation: Jeffrey Swartz
© of this edition:
Editorial Tenov
Casp 147
08013 Barcelona
tenov@editorialtenov.com
www.tenovbooks.com

Design by TENOV
Printed in L'Automàtica and Bookprint, Barcelona

ISBN: 978-84-939231-7-4
DL:B-17901-2015

This one people [the Sumerians] *held such exact and superior*
force that all peoples around them were sustained by it,
nourished, increased, advanced, that a city was a coherence
which, for the first time since the ice, gave man the chance to
join knowledge to culture and, with this weapon, shape dignities
of economics and value sufficient to make daily life itself a
dignity and a sufficiency.

Charles Olson*

---

* Poet Charles Olson (1910-1970) was the author of some of the first performance art in
history, together with John Cage and Merce Cunningham. His poetic writing is at the
origin of modernist movements like beat poetry, lettrism, Situationism and Fluxus.

TABLE OF CONTENTS

THE HOUSE

AESTHETICS

LAY OF THE LAND

Prologue

A cornerstone was an essential feature of ancient architecture. Before beginning construction a foundational ritual was performed where the earth was blessed and an offering made. Afterwards, trenches were dug in the ground where the first stones or bricks would be laid for the building's foundation. Once in place, these cornerstones determined the size and shape of the building to be erected. More than simple foundation stones, they seemed to be the very source of the future structure. The stones established the surface area to be taken away from the powers of the earth and the underworld. They were necessary for any construction project, since the history of their creators was inscribed in them, whether they were gods, heroes or simple human beings.

The Mesopotamian culture that emerged in the Tigris and Euphrates Delta thousands of years ago is often presented to us nowadays as dead, distant and largely incomprehensible. Nonetheless, our perception of the world and many of our beliefs have Mesopotamian roots. The texts of classical Greece and the Bible resound with its myths, which brings it, even if just for a moment, that much closer to us.

Perhaps this is simply an illusion. We can never know what men really thought ten millennia ago, or what criteria they used to arrange their world. Mesopotamian culture was not rediscovered until the nineteenth century. What emerges from the study of the vestiges found are not so much the voices of the past but our own concerns, which seem to want to seek out some sort of grounding in the texts of a distant culture. Our interpretation of the indicators they left behind is based on our knowledge, as we turn the past into a creation inevitably reflecting our own points of view, into something as pertinent as contemporary creation itself.

This set of articles and notes on the idea of the city delves into the past with the idea of finding answers addressing questions belonging to the present. The city was the most important of Mesopotamia's contributions, since it altered social and economic structures as well as conceptual perspectives of the world. The first cities, arising as they did during the fifth millennium BC, were not isolated cases. Thanks to the transportation links uniting them, they were able to weave themselves into a network that would irreversibly modify the territory.

In trying to understand the origin of a transformational process that has come down to our day, it is interesting to explore the past in order to find out just what these cities were like, who their first architects were (whether real or mythical), what structures were built and what aesthetic ideas they were based on.

In this way, by perpetuating an earlier era of gods and heroes, our world is enriched by new interpretational perspectives resting firmly upon a solid cornerstone, the cultural foundation of the edifice we seek to raise.

Acknowledgments

This group of texts brings together contributions from experts and artists whose information and corrections I am thankful for. All the same, any errors that might appear should be attributed entirely to myself.

I would like to thank Jordi Abadal, Béatrice André-Salvini, Joan Aruz, Zainab Bahrani, Marcel Borràs, Carmen Cantarell, Amira Edan, Geoff Emberling, Lluis Feliu, Victoria Garriga, Lledó Gas, Jean-Louis Huot, Gregorio Luri, Jean-Claude Margueron, Maria-Grazia Masetti-Rouault, Maria Gabriella Micale, Piotr Michalowski (in his double role as Sumerologist and experimental free jazz composer-performer, an extraordinary model for taking on the past), Adelina Millet, Béatrice Müller, Gregorio del Olmo, Miguel Orellana, Jennifer Pournelle, Olivier Rouault, Gonzalo Rubio, Eric Rusiñol, Joaquín Sanmartín, Julia Schulz-Dornburg and Norman Yoffee.

I cannot forget that this exploration began when the publishers (who are also my friends) Gustavo Gili and later Mónica Gili accepted the proposal to publish my first studies on Mesopotamia, encouraging knowledge of a culture we have come to believe has the power to speak in present-day voices.

In the same way, I would like to express my deepest gratitude to the Gerda Henkel Foundation in Düsseldorf, for the grant given to me along with Marcel Borràs, Albert Imperial and Marc Marín (the "Sumer Team"), along with the permission and aid of the University of Bagdad (special thanks to Doctor Ghada Siliq), the University of Samawa and the Directorate General of Antiquities of Iraq, which authorized us to visit and study Sumerian sites in the country, altering and enriching our vision of the Sumerian world, bringing it closer to our own day and age. We do not so much travel back to the founts of culture, but rather reveal them to the present so as to better perceive them from our own, more modern perspective.

My most recent research on Sumerian architecture and cities was done in preparation for the exhibition *Before the Flood: Mesopotamia, 3500-2100 BC,* which I curated for the Fundació "la Caixa" in Spain. I am particularly grateful to them for that opportunity.

I would also like to thank Jennifer Y. Chi for giving me the possibility to continue to study Mesopotamian organization of space, and to think about the meaning of Mesopotamian "arts and crafts" today (if any). I am also thankful to her for the exhibition we curated together, with the assistance of Marc Marín, *Past and Present: Archaeology and Aesthetics*, at the Institute for the Study of the Ancient World (ISAW), New York, 2015.

A number of articles published over a period of two years in my blog (*Tochoocho*, or *T8*, "Eighth Brick" in English, at www.tochoocho.blogspot) are the source of these texts, though they have been fully revised for publication here. I am aware that any essay, however short, on early Mesopotamian "art theory", has to deal with texts and artifacts that may have different functions, goals and meanings, belonging as they do to very different periods, separated by millennia. I have tried, if possible, to focus on written and graphic data from central and southern Mesopotamia, from the third and early second millennia BC.

I would like, in closing, to express my gratitude to publishers Llorenç Bonet and Joana Teixidor for their interest and commitment in giving me the opportunity to publish in Tenov, with its beautifully produced books. I thank them as well for all their suggestions and corrections, arranging chapters and the book itself, ordering and improving the text. Thanks to them another of my dreams has come true.

THE CITY

The (Imaginary) Origin of the City

Specialists continue to research the reasons leading to the emergence of the city in the fourth millennium BC in a region as unstable as the Tigris and Euphrates Delta. They have sought to demonstrate that urban structures also appeared, almost simultaneously, in the Indus Valley in Central Asia, though their results are inconclusive. Sumerian culture is the first to have the city represent the center of life, both mythologically and in reality.

Writing, royalty, the creation of a permanent army and irrigation canals are other features of civilization that appear simultaneously with urban life, as seen for the first time in Sumer. This is why great effort has been made to show they are related. Agriculture in a parched desert, far from the fertile banks of the rivers, had need of irrigation, so it was necessary to lay out a network of canals. A construction project of that size required a strong government able to plan over a wide territory, then carry out the work and defend it from attackers charging down from the high steppes of Asia. At the same time, the fair distribution of water and the harvest made it necessary to have a system of calculation and annotation.

Nevertheless, all these highly convincing theories have been undone. It has not been possible to find a single cause to explain the appearance of the social and spatial structures of the city that are still dominant today.

Quite logically, the first myths we know of are Sumerian, as they are the first to be recorded (the Egyptians invented their writing a short time afterwards). These myths tell of the lives of the gods and thus establish the existence of the first known religious pantheons in history. It has often been thought that such pantheons, presided over by the higher gods, reflected human social organizations under the tutelage of a king, a priestly caste and an army. In this way, the world of the gods would be the ideal image (however distorted) of the lives of men, forged as it was to legitimize certain social structures.

Space plays an important role in Sumerian mythology. The gods, with An at the forefront, lived in palaces found in cities—real cities—at a time preceding that of men. These palaces were magnificently complex constructions that would be impossible to find on earth. Some were in the sky and others under water; they were built with quality materials (precious metals, ivory, fine wood) and adorned with shimmering jewels. They had towers as high as mountain peaks; their intricate interiors were perfectly designed and magically lit, with labyrinthic floor plans resembling the weave of finely worked cloth; their gardens were luxuriant. The habitat of the gods had nothing to do with the human environment, and its perfection and complexity could not be realized on earth. The palaces of An, Enlil and Enki recall the futuristic constructions found in the novels of Jules Verne.

The cities of the future, described by countless fictional writers of the nineteenth and twentieth centuries, are based on real cities, though teeming with unrealizable inventions. A myriad of vehicles slice through the skies past vertiginously high buildings, tracing multi-level freeways at dizzying heights. Years or centuries later, these dreams (or nightmares) would end up becoming real. The thousand-yard-high skyscrapers now being built in Dubai, Shanghai or Chicago would have been quite enough to satisfy the wildest science fiction fantasies of the last century.

So what came first? Was it the "earthly" city, from which the city of the gods was conceived? Or were the divine dwelling places described by the poets later "imitated" on earth? Various Sumerian chronicles and myths tell of how the city and the kings had descended from heaven in the period before the flood. Myths tend to tell the truth, in a more or less imaginative way.

Thus the reason for the rise of the city and all required structures for controlling its surroundings could be found in the myths and legends fashioned over centuries and even millennia of oral tradition. These fictional tales told of brightly perfect worlds, invented to withstand the pressure of hostile surroundings. Such fictions would have required the invention of some sort of system of transmission and fixation, as would be the case with writing.

It is possible that one day humans will feel capable of building on earth what is recited in the bards' tales. The city would be a dream become reality, and if that were the case, in the beginning there would be the imagination.

Cult and the City

The city emerges in Mesopotamia in the Bronze Age, between 5000 BC and 3500 BC. Until then, and ever since the beginning of the Neolithic Period (between 12000 BC and 9000 BC), there had only been villages, though it was possible for a single village to have a considerable number of dwellings. These villages were comprised of self-sufficient family or clan units of comparable sizes that would then unite, perhaps to facilitate matrimonial ties and ensure better defense systems for the villagers and their possessions. In the city, in contrast, houses had different sizes, reflecting social stratification. From the palace all the way down to the hut there lived kings, courtesans, chiefs, priests, military officials and craftspeople. Specialized buildings stood out above the rest, a natural consequence of the division of labor, and included religious sites, palaces, workshops and warehouses.

Various reasons have been given for the material and social transformation of villages into cities, or for why cities were founded on virgin territories. The need to control greater areas of agricultural land to meet rising needs for food supply led to social and urban reorganization. Such transformations could not have taken place without strong government, sanctified by the heavens, backed by a committed army and able to control anyone producing goods. Writing as well tends to be understood as a tool arising in parallel to the city, so as to administer and control the flow of products between the country and town and thus manage emerging markets. This explanation cannot always be demonstrated, as archaeological discoveries fail to consistently corroborate it. It is not even true that the earliest examples of writing were always for accounting purposes.

Twenty-five years ago the Hellenist scholar François de Polignac published a polemical hypothesis, now largely accepted. He described how the plan of the ancient Greek city did not always correspond to a previously conceived layout, but rather to the evolution of the earliest religious processions. In the Greek colonies in the south of Italy and Sicily (known as Magna Graecia) the recently arrived settlers participated in important pilgrimages from the temples of the nascent city to an outlying ring of holy sites. These religious destinations were often found in places the native population considered to be traditionally sacred. Since they were set off from the new cities they ended up serving as a veritable line of defense for the urban space, which in this way had no need to be fortified. Thus the urban structure did not arise from an externally imposed geometric model, but was determined by the religious sentiment certain sites aroused, inspiring the faithful along paths that would eventually become the city's first streets.

Attributing the foundation of Greek colonial cities to processional rites and not to economic or social needs made it easier to understand the motivation bringing humans together: the cult around a divinity. This complex yet common task brought them to live together and jointly delegate certain functions and powers to others. This religious motivation could perhaps be further applied to the very foundation of the idea of urban space. In Greece and in Etruria, in the center of Italy, there were urban leagues, associations of cities that came together on the basis of a shared cult to the same god.

Ceremony, communion and sacred foodstuffs gave these groups their common identity. A shared cult could also explain how human beings chose to join together and create a habitat of a new formal and social type: the city. The city would be organized in function of the necessities of ritual, where a priestly class would be required to instruct in its guidelines, while other social strata would be needed to produce and protect religious offerings: soldiers, farmers and artisans.

Relationships amongst these new urban dwellers were visually symbolized by what makes up a city, a network of transportation routes, public space and functionally differentiated buildings. The city was conceived so its citizens could get to their places of worship. All roads lead to the heart of Rome.

In this way, then, a transcendent impulse, however marked by venial desires, would have pushed humans to reconsider their ways of life so as to find the best way to divide up between them and share the attention certain gods might require.

The needs that led to the creation of the city were not just material, but spiritual. The city should therefore be looked upon as more of a superhuman construction than one related to natural existence.

Settlement

Uru (or *iri*) is the most habitual Sumerian word for "city", though it is not the only one. Other compound terms reveal what image the Mesopotamians had of their settlements.

The action of settlement could be designated by the expression $dur_2...\hat{g}ar$. It turns out that $\hat{g}ar$ is a term that can be translated as a noun ("place") or a verb ("to deploy", "to spread out"). Thus to say "to settle" they said something like "place to deploy or spread oneself out." Yet it could also be dangerous to settle in any place whatsoever.

The word for town or small city was *eduru* or e_2-$duru_5$. E_2 is translated as "house", but also as "temple". It is employed to refer to any permanent residence, whether for a man or a god. More precisely, it was used to refer to a home rather than a house in the architectural sense. Dur_2, as we have seen, is translated as "to settle" or "to sit". A town is thus a place where it is possible to settle (or sit down) in trust. It is only possible to rest when you feel secure and can let your guard down. E_2-dur_2 is a space that surrounds you and gives you a welcoming feeling of wellbeing, a permanent home.

Besides the term e_2, it was also possible to say *ma* for "house". *Ma* became part of the compound term *ma-da*, where together with *ma* we find *da* or *dag*, "side" or "neighborhood". The term refers to something nearby, to what is close. *Ma-da* is "earth", but not in an abstract sense; it is earth conceived as a welcoming place, where a person feels like he or she is being accompanied. Earth then emerges as something close to us, something familiar we can trust.

Architecture has the function of symbolizing the ties human beings make with space, seen as something beneficial, as something to be shared with those close to us. Only the stranger looks for shelter out in the open.

From Town to City

The differences between a town and a city have not been precisely delineated. Historians, archeologists and anthropologists studying the Middle East continue to discuss the characteristics (whether physical or human) a town must acquire for it to be considered a city.

Size is not primordial, so that a city need not necessarily have more inhabitants than a town. On the other hand, what indicates the shift from one to the other are division of labor, the accumulation of goods in certain hands and both social and architectural hierarchy, as seen in the size of buildings and the lavishness of tombs.

Jean-Louis Huot masterfully sets out a final distinguishing characteristic. A town is comprised of a community of laborers working with their hands: smiths, potters, bricklayers, and so on. These craftsmen live in their workplace and pay particular attention to their tools. A city brings together such craftsmen as well, but they no longer make a living from what they do: they live from what they preach. The word works together with the product or even substitutes it. What is useful in and of itself is nothing if it does not come along with a discourse to espouse its virtues and hide its imperfections. Its coming is proclaimed, though what exists only in the form of its prior announcement is treated as if it were already here.

Besides this, the city brings together inhabitants who live solely by the word. Priests, kings, legislators and teachers are men who do not produce anything tangible. The city is a space for the commerce of goods and ideas. The public square, where everything is proclaimed, offered and exposed, substitutes the craftsman's workshop. Rituals, in contrast, take place in the countryside or on the outskirts of cities, where the main holy sites are found: in the terrain of the annunciation, of the word proclaiming the one and only truth. The city, in contrast, is teeming with advertisement, images and illusions without a necessary correlation to "reality". It is the site of fiction.

Plato understood perfectly what a city consisted of. It was the space where charlatans and tricksters moved about at will, proclaiming what likely did not exist and pretending to be what they were not when performing in the public space. Plato sought to construct an impossible structure, a city where *apate*—trickery—and *pseudos*—lies, tall tales—might be proscribed. The Platonic republic could only exist in the imagination; it was a contradiction in terms.

It was not by chance that Corinth, the great port and merchant city of Archaic Greece, had a temple dedicated to Aphrodite, or that the center of the agora was presided by an image of Peitho, goddess of Persuasion. It was the city where everything was up for grab, from the goods it produced to the bodies of the celebrated priestesses in the service of Aphrodite.

The city is the space of the future, full bent on gathering what is still pending and perhaps will never come, replaced by the word announcing it. Its mere promise is quite enough. Indeed, if this future were ever to materialize we would be disappointed, our desire quashed, and the city would lose its *raison d'être*.

The Artist, the Artisan and the City

A long time ago craftsmen making tools for the tribe lived and worked in dark, thick-walled huts on the outskirts of the village, somewhere at the edge of the woods.

Their days were spent with hardly any contact with other villagers, who in turn both relied on them and feared them. They were superior beings, clearly enough, as they enticed the earth into opening up its veins to them to extract what they most desired. They would stoke a fire in the middle of the workshop, reaching temperatures for the founding and transmutation of metals, which with Herculean strength they then tempered. They turned wet clay into something harder, dry and sound like stone. They even accomplished the most astonishing metamorphosis of all: in their fires a material as dull and elusive as sand was transformed into something viscous and transparent. Simply by blowing air into it could it be expanded and shaped into a vessel as lucent as chilly water.

Those who lorded over the elements, transforming them into every imaginable shape, had to be magicians, assisted by dark, supernatural powers. Their very appearance, with their faces sweaty and reddened by the fire, their titanic limbs sculpted by years handling the tongs, raised them (so the myths would say) to the heights of ancient deities, or just as well to the echelon of spirits from some diabolical land.

The fire they lived with, as Vitruvius observed, was the reason they had to set themselves off from the center of town, while the tribe's fortune and survival continued to depend upon the success of their diligent labor.

Thousands of years went by, and the towns became cities. Power passed from the hands of the elders to those who were strongest, to the most astute, to the cruelest amongst them, who with luck on their side would rule: kings and priests took control over the new urban centers. In imposing their dictates they had need of a caste of young soldiers, a blindly obedient military class whose task was to submit the townspeople day in and day out, having transformed themselves (in the people's eyes) into the representatives of the will of celestial gods.

In order to allow kings and priests to live shut up inside their palaces and holy places, and to ensure the soldiers did not turn against them, the rest of the population had to work. Somebody had to labor the land, planting and irrigating the crops and taking care of domesticated livestock, so the markets would be well stocked. Others had to create the tools needed for life at court. Then there was a final group required to make the images the priests and monarchs needed to honor their insatiable, wrathful gods, or to build monumental sites for both the living and the dead. They were needed to impress both one's own population and one's enemies, who when faced with such a great show of might would retreat in fear. In this way a third caste appeared whose work continued to awe, however much their fortune had changed.

The emergence of the socially-stratified city destroyed the power of the artisans. They had been pure magicians, holding sway over invisible powers; they had been feared and respected. The life and death of the town, with its handful of buildings housing self-sufficient clans, had been quite literally in their hands.

The royal, priestly and military estates at the head of the social hierarchy of the city also relied on the services of artisans and other producers. Yet these latter were no longer honored or feared, and instead were forced to work, enslaved. They could now be sold or replaced, and at any moment their sustenance could be cut off. Having become interchangeable pawns in submission to the whims and caprice of the city governors, they no longer inspired fear.

The artisans, however, did not just resign themselves to their newfound ill fortune. Already in times of Alexander certain painters and sculptors sought to restore the prestige that had been wrested from them. They had the ability to extol the image of the monarch in their work, creating resemblances of his face or just as well mocking it, knowing full well that either choice could seal their fate.

More than a thousand years later the artisans reawakened to claim what was theirs. They did not want to be treated as mere marionettes. Just like the wizards of old, they too wielded surprising powers. Their art was proof of their semi-divine virtues, of their genius. They were able to create deceptively real effigies, lacking only the breath of life itself (something that later on, with automatons, would not even be missing). Like the alchemists, they transformed matter. Their secret processes enabled them to create pigments whose tones were unseen in nature. They were wise men, like the priests, designing inscrutable emblems. They were able to conceive of and erect a building where nothing was left to chance, as if it were the direct and precise materialization of a dream.

Yet the artisans were no longer as necessary as they had previously been. Their job would be to come up with distractions to make the authorities seem even more powerful, while taking the edge off any negative traits. Yet life in the metropolis no longer depended on them doing their job well.

They tried to draw attention to themselves, ostentatiously or grotesquely. They painted and sculpted increasingly unusual images and portraits; they made proclamations; they defecated in public; they sold their excrement for the price of gold; they mutilated themselves; they claimed to be the guardians of truth. Furthermore, they acquired large sums of money; museums were built for them and they were showered with gold. They were guests at the banquets of the powerful. Yet the doubt remains as to whether they were (or are) little more than fools, keeping the people's minds elsewhere, far from what really moves the city.

Artists, like magicians powerful enough to change the world, could only have existed before the founding of the city. As soon as urban order was imposed, they became producers of mirrors, which only in the best case scenario could timidly or temporarily alter the existing order, before being condemned or expelled as Plato had wished.

The magic of art has no place in the city, and cities, what is more, are needed to conceive the world. Art as a transforming power in the world is a utopia we are only too happy to believe in.

The Size of the City

In the early period the Sumerians used annotations of dots and lines to write numbers. Later they recurred to cuneiform signs, just as they did for writing. Nevertheless, the monosyllabic sounds of these signs also designated other things, and each sign could have various readings.

The number seven, for example, was written with a sign that was read as *imin*. Yet *imin* could also be broken down into *ia$_2$*, five, and *min$_3$*, two. The very name of the number seven contained the sum of numbers giving rise to it. Seven, in Sumerian, was said "five-two".

However, it was also the case that *ia$_2$* was a verb that meant "to win a battle", and *min$_3$* (or *mana*) referred to a fellow soldier. In this way the number seven was the number of victory, and this was why the weapons and defensive systems of a city had to have seven parts.

Another example was that the structure of the triumphant heavens, as the perfect dwelling place of the gods, were seen to have seven tiers.

The Mesopotamian numerical system was sexagesimal (with base sixty), and certain numbers were associated with divinities. As the supreme deity, An, god of the heavens, had to contain the basic units: the number sixty. In turn his favorite son, Enlil, had a lower value, and was represented by the number fifty.

Each city was associated with a founding deity who watched over it. Quite often the city had the same name as its protector god, as was the case of Asur, the capital of Assyria, which bore the name of its pantheon's principal deity. The names of cities had various readings, since each syllable of a name could have a numerical equivalent. On the other hand, the sum of the figures "contained" in the name of the city had to correspond to the number associated with its deity.

The first Sumerian cities were not newly founded, but were the result of the merging of nearby preexisting towns from the Neolithic period. This is what, as applied to Greece, was known as synoecism: the union of towns and markets with common interests and beliefs. In contrast, the

Neo-Assyrian emperors in the first millennium did indeed set about founding cities and colonies on virgin lands.

The city's name was not a chance affair, as it indicated the measurement of the city's perimeter. The name, therefore, offered a clue to imagining what the built city was like. Urban plans, in this sense, were unnecessary, given that the numbers needed to plan and build the city were already contained in its name. The name thus prefigured the city, invoking the deity, and was immediately materialized in the forms it would be constructed in. No king would have dared to build without divine approval, and no monarch could choose a name for a city, for its name was everything.

City architects had to be erudite, and the creation of the city was authentically poetic, for it gave primacy to the word—the divine word where numerical perfection shone brightly, as numbers made it possible to arrange the world.

The City as an Island

Sumerian archaeological remains can hardly be recognized in our day in the midst of the desert, where they blend in with the surrounding dunes. However, recent studies made possible by the first permits to visit Iraq in thirty years, allow us to conclude that the first cities in the south of Mesopotamia, such as Uruk, Ur, Lagash and Eridu, were founded in the wetland landscape of the Tigris and Euphrates Delta.

The delta is slowly recovering after a rather aggressive program to drain it undertaken by Saddam Hussein in the 1990s. It is comprised of a dense network of natural channels flowing around countless mounds of solid reed sediments, their ground holding firm.

The land where various peoples lived in the fifth and fourth millennia BC, speaking Sumerian, Akkadian, Elamite and other languages, was a large plain with marshy patches. Each tribe or town was part of a larger group, with the parts both separated from and connected to each other along the river channels. The settlements were laid out in accordance with the irregular structure of the river meanders and the delta itself. This geography implied that the cities could not put down deep roots. They seemed to rise out of the waters, floating upon them. Proof of this is that a verb translated as "to settle" also meant "to suspend".

An island is a piece of land emerging from the waters, suggesting birth or rebirth. In many origin myths, whether in Egypt, Mesopotamia or Greece, life begins after the earliest land arises from out of the Primal Waters. Apollo, for example, the Greek god of territorial organization, was born on the island of Delos. An island is a piece of land surrounded on all sides by water, and for this reason needs to have contact with other islands, so as to make up "isles" of civilization. This was the case of Delos, head of the Delian League.

The cities were islands connected by lines of communication, a network structure that was not only formal but social as well. All cities were equally important, and no single city dominated the rest. The only possible exception was Eridu, a small settlement whose relevance was not based on its size or number of inhabitants, but on the fact that it was home to the main sanctuary of Enki. This was how Eridu came to be prestigious, its status far exceeding its physical dimension.

The image of an area made up of islands no doubt determined the physiognomy of cities and urban networks when marking out the territory; they were at the mercy of the whimsical waters, yet played with them as well. Still today in languages like Spanish one speaks of *islas* (islands) when referring to large blocks of urban housing units separated from others by streets.

This physical and mental organization ended when the coastline pushed out and the waters went with it. The cities, in spite of being crisscrossed by rivers and channels, were no longer surrounded by water. The territorial structure changed as the land was divided into lots and separations were made. With such alterations society began to arrange itself more hierarchically. The first empires ruled by deified kings were founded, coinciding with the first stepped pyramids, the ziggurats. A new era began, which perhaps was already our own.

Imagination and Space

The first southern Mesopotamian cities were settled on countless islands made from compressed reeds and separated by natural channels. This is why, from the fifth to the third millennium BC, in parallel to the development of cities, there was a growth in transportation links on land, rivers and the sea, creating an expanded network covering the entire plain running from present-day Bagdad to the coastal waters.

The network was so important in the second half of the third millennium BC that a king like Shulgi, considered a god on earth, was even prouder of his accomplishments in setting up transportation links (including canals and roads) than of the cities and temples he had built.

Sumerian myths and hymns tell of numerous journeys taking their heroes to nearby cities, or just as well to the furthest reaches of the earth. The same gods were always moving about: Inanna the goddess of fertility and destruction travelled down to the very heart of the underworld. Even when the gods were materialized in cult statues, they were taken from temple to temple during annual processions to visit their divine relatives.

Nature had the image of slow, perpetual movement. The slimy waters of the Tigris and the Euphrates moved lethargically and majestically, winding along drawn out bends, never seeming to reach the sea. The tall vegetation in the marshes was constantly agitated by breezes whispering through the reeds, as described in the epic tale of Gilgamesh. This constant flow constituted an ideal state, the much-desired condition of life.

The city-states were almost always in conflict. Even so, it seems that cunning more than violence governed urban relationships. No single city seemed to want to have control of the territory. The odd skirmish, frequent pacts and a few sieges set the tone of their shared existence. It does not seem they ever felt obliged to fight all-out wars. The cities were rivals, though at least until the end of the third millennium no single one of them seemed concerned about putting an end to the rest.

City-states were more likely to pursue treaty agreements between each other. In the Sumerian imagination, human beings were merely visitors on earth, they were not its children. This is quite the opposite of what is seen in certain Greek cities later on, or with the identification between earth and blood that has set the tone in Europe from the nineteenth century until our day; the Sumerians, in contrast, did not believe their roots ran deep. They did not consider themselves to be settlers sprouting out from the earth, nor believed they held all possible rights over the land for that reason alone. For the Sumerians, the most important thing was to bring the other in, to establish solid ties between different communities.

Dialogue, playfulness and trickery, rather than political, religious or ethnic violence, were the instruments used to manage intercity relationships. Although almost all the cities were surrounded by walls, the function of such fortifications was more symbolic than defensive. In the fifth millennium there was no clan powerful and large enough to threaten a city as immense and important as Uruk. The wall allowed the inhabitants to feel proud of being members of a potent community that was recognizable from a distance. Their symbolic idea was that those dwelling there had decided to share a space of common interest. Urban social organization was regulated by blending in instead of by exclusion.

The first cities were not divided into specialized neighborhoods. As they were not segregated for reasons of social class, nobles and artisans shared urban space. Even though their houses were distinct, social and professional classes did tend to mix.

Today more than ever we should turn our gaze towards Sumer, if there is still time left to do so.

THE ARCHITECTS

Enki Built on the Waters

Enki, the Sumerian god of architecture, controlled the immense marshes of the Tigris and Euphrates Delta, whose murky waters were held to be the semen of the fertilizing divinity. Along the shores of the rivers was found the holy city of Eridu, and Enki was its protecting god.

The marshes were conceived as Primal Waters, where the gods emerged at the beginning of the world's creation. These divine waters were known as Abzu, meaning "wise waters". In their depths was found the palace of Enki, and upon them floated the great sanctuary dedicated to him.

At that time Enki had full control of the waters, both those that flowed and those that were still. The mother of the waters of knowledge was called Id, the Primal River. Abzu and Id were related to Nammu, mother of Enki, whose name means "womb". In this way, the waters were the source of all things: conceived as a receptacle of life, they watered the earth with the gift they bore, the fertile slime.

Enki was not the world's creator but rather its organizer. He was able to place all things created by the Heavens in the right place, thanks to his word. He channeled the flow of the matriarchal waters and set out the limit of each feature, carefully ensuring the waters did not rise up from the river bed and destroy life on solid ground.

Each city had its own principal god, with the majority related to An, the god of heaven, Enlil, god of the air and of the water that falls from the sky, and Enki, god of the earth and of groundwater, of rivers and marshes. The city of Girsu was protected by Ningirsu, god of cultivated land, an agrarian deity with dominion over the proper division of lands and the plowing of fields. Ningirsu had the task of controlling the waters, making it possible for the plowed and sown land to be fertile. In the autobiography of the Neo-Sumerian monarch Gudea, King of Lagash, we read:

$\hat{G}e_{26}$ ^{d}nin-ĝir$_2$-su a huš gi$_4$-a
Gudea Cylinder A, IX, 20

That is, the god Ningirsu closed off the frightening waters, which caused fear when spilling over, leading to destructive flooding. The verb gi_4 literally means "to surround", "to close" or "to lay siege to"; it had to do with turning around and making things return, quite literally, to their course.

Oddly enough, this verse is identical to one from the Biblical Psalms, from the well-known verses on the splendors of God's creation where the constructive actions of Yahweh are laid out in detail:

> He lays the beams of his chambers on the waters.
> Psalm 104:3

> The waters fled...to the place you assigned for them. You set a boundary they cannot cross; never again will they cover the earth.
> Psalm 104:7-9

As with Ningirsu and Enki—or better said, like the Mesopotamian gods of creation and order—Yahweh controlled the waters, setting out their place and enclosing them. In spite of the qualms Old Testament writers had about builders, who were descended from Cain, Yahweh behaved as a veritable architect, placing the sources of life at the service of men and making sure they did not get out of control. Making architecture means giving shape to what is shapeless, and water has, by definition, the most elusive of shapes.

And the King Surrounded Them

In an official letter written on a clay tablet, the great Babylonian king Hammurabi presented himself as the Lord of the Four Regions of the World (a title he was customarily known by). Hammurabi then laid out the achievements of his reign, emphasizing the walls made of earth and dust, high as craggy mountain ranges, whose upper reaches stood out proudly. Amongst these and other feats he mentioned the following:

> Ambar-ra hu-mu-ni-nigin$_2$
> Kalamazoo Valley Museum (KVM) 32.1197, v.14

This phrase tends to be translated as "he surrounded the walls of his city with a moat full of water." The activity of digging canals and keeping them in good condition was quite habitual in Mesopotamia, whether to irrigate land or control flooding. In this way they would imitate the work undertaken by Enki after the creation of the universe.

The use of the term *ambar*, which means "swamp" or "marsh", is rather unusual. It reflects the massive areas of calm, reed-ridden water in the Tigris and Euphrates Delta, where the city of Sippar in the text is found. We might imagine that the moat protecting the city walls was full of murky water teeming with reeds.

The original letter was written in the Akkadian language. However, the previous quotations come from a translation into Sumerian that was likely done in the same court, and does not read quite the same as the original Akkadian. Perhaps this is due to the inexperience of the translator, who was overly literal, as the translation says "go around the waters". It is not an accusative case but ablative. The phrase could be interpreted as "he undertakes the action of surrounding the waters", that is, "he surrounds the waters." If this were the case, then, the waters would not be surrounding the wall, but would be themselves encircled.

Many specialists believe that the term *ambar* is an incorrect reading of a cuneiform sign that should be read as *abbar*, where *ab* means "water". In this way, then, *abbar* would be translated as "sea" or "ocean", and *ambar*, as cited in the letter, would not refer to a reed-infested, freshwater moat, but to sea water. In this latter case, then, what Hammurabi accomplished was to surround not a wall or a canal, but the sea itself.

This interpretation of the description recalls the verse from the Book of Job, where the wisdom of God lays out the greatness of the Creator's works:

> He has drawn a circle on the waters.
> Job 26:10

This would be just one more example of how much the Bible owes to Mesopotamia. It could be somewhat exaggerated to compare human works to divine ones, though it does allow us to conceive of a symbolic reading of Hammurabi's text.

Quite probably this letter should not be taken literally, which would be the case with the majority of royal writings. It does not give us an exact account of the king's endeavors. Perhaps it would be better to say that it tells the truth, though on a symbolic rather than historical level. Royal letters, like mythical texts, announce paradigmatic actions that tend to show the king's grandeur, his pious relationship with the gods. Not every king would set out to dredge canals, raise walls or rebuild temples. Some did so, while others simply told of such things, so as to live on in posterity. The simple fact of stating something evoked grandeur, even if the feats mentioned had never perhaps been accomplished.

In this case, royal greatness would be based on an improbable idea, set quite beyond the limits of the imagination, beyond what could be reasonably dreamt: laying siege to the sea. The image is powerful, evoking the magnificence of Hammurabi, who was capable of acting like the gods as he rearranged the world. The king would have accomplished the mighty feat of building upon the sea. So that the omnipotence of the monarch was expressed by means of an architectural gesture, as would have been so typically the case.

The Heavens are on Bricks

The expression "the vaults of heaven" shows how various cultures conceived the celestial firmament as architectural. In Mesopotamia the gods lived in a palace floating in the sky. However, this was not a prototype but rather the image of the original habitable space. The Primal Waters, called Abzu, were thought of as an aquatic mansion with various rooms in a massive enclosure.

The celestial palace, the result of the projection of the House of Water in Heaven, worked simultaneously as a model of the earthly temple of the divinity. In the Babylonian tradition, the supreme god Marduk followed Abzu's plans to build the great sky-bound temple of Esarra for An, Enlil and Enki. Later on, Marduk built his own mansion on earth, imitating Esarra, the Babylonian city he was to reign, where Esagil the earthly temple was particularly prominent.

This three-part division of things, with an original earthly model and a first, heavenly copy, which in turn would be the model for the second material version, is also found in the Bible. In effect, Yahweh dwelt in a celestial palace, found in the heart of the city in the air, the celestial Jerusalem, which in turn was made from a prototype, the Garden of Eden. The palace was then projected onto the earth so as to give form to the earthly temple, the Temple of Jerusalem, which bore resemblance to Paradise. In both cases, the space where it all began was projected in antithetical directions in space until coming up with clearly defined celestial and earthly structures.

It has been said that the notion of celestial architecture had little importance in Greece. Only a few examples of it can be found in the archaic and classical periods. The best known is one of the first mythical temples to Apollo in Delphos, built out of feathers and hovering in the air.

Plato refers on two occasions to the existence of celestial architectures. In the *Republic*, dedicated to the structure of a model city, he writes:

No city could ever be blessed unless its lineaments were traced [*diagrapheian*] by artists [*chromenoi dzographoi*] who used the heavenly model [*theio paradeigmati*].
Republic, Book 6, 500e

Further along in a commentary on how nowhere in the world (except in the text) can a state be found as perfect as that described, he says:

Perhaps there is a pattern [*paradeigma*] of it laid up in heaven [*ouranoo*] for him who wishes to contemplate it and so beholding to constitute himself its citizen.
Republic, Book 9, 592b

In Mesopotamia the relationship between the model, reality and the image determines that primacy belongs to an original, terrestrial being, while in Greece the model is celestial. Plato adds that the author of the constitution meant to regulate community life should consider men, but should also pay attention to what is above, where the essence of justice, beauty, temperance, and other similar virtues resides.

This relationship between what is on high and what is down low could recall how things worked in Mesopotamia. Plato, however, uses the term *phusis* to name the model, and *phusis* means above all "the action of giving birth". The celestial paradigm is not only light, but also illuminates material reality, presented as what has come down from the idea, a familial relationship that implies a close resemblance to the model.

Plato emphasized the primacy of the celestial, the progenitor of what is terrestrial. Celestial architectures and buildings were "essential": the cities and buildings humans inhabit would have no "reason to be" if it were not for the necessarily previous existence of heavenly cities and architectures. This concept is in the origin of Western architecture, and especially so from the sixteenth century Platonic revival onwards.

The First Female Architect

The Dream of King Gudea is part of a long composition in verse where the king explains the steps he had taken to obey the orders of the protecting deity Ningirsu, as spoken to him in a dream. His task was to build the main temple of his city, Lagash. The text was written with cuneiform signs on three large terracotta cylinders, only two of which have survived, now in the Louvre. There are only a few translations of what is no doubt the first architect's statement in history.

The tale begins with a dream where Ningirsu makes contact with his protected one Gudea, showing him a scene where a number of gods intervene. When he wakes up, Gudea is unable to interpret the dream, so he goes to his mother's temple, where he explains his vision to the goddess Nanshe. Gudea explains how a female figure appeared before him, carrying a lapis lazuli tablet with the plan for a temple Ningirsu had ordered to be built. Nanshe reveals the name of the female figure to the bewildered Gudea: it is the goddess Nisaba, who is described in the following way:

> Saĝ-ĝá è ki garadin₉ mu-ak
> Gudea Cylinder A, IV, 24

This could be interpreted as something in the line of "Nisaba makes sheaves from ears of wheat gathered from the ground." The meaning is so uncertain that the only way to make sense of it is by forcing the grammar; quite logically it is often left untranslated. The meaning of the ears of wheat is not clear; nor can we comprehend the reason the goddess Nisaba gathers them, especially given that at the same time she is holding two small tablets. On her lap there is the tablet of the stars, while in her hand she holds a second lapis lazuli tablet, where the plan of the temple has been inscribed. Even though the verse is not that clear, it does allow us to lay out a heterogeneous set of objects related to Nisaba: the wheat, the awl she writes with and the tablets themselves.

It could be said that Nisaba was the personification of cultivated grain crops. They were not only gathered and transported by the goddess, but (as a number of depictions show) the ears of wheat sprang from her body as well. A Mesopotamian hymn depicts Nisaba as the daughter of the earth; another likens her to a maternal goddess; yet another associates her with the underworld, as life springs forth from the earth and returns to it.

The physical welfare of a human being depended upon Nisaba, it was born from her. She is the goddess who watches over the fields of grain, the one who gives them sustenance. The ears of wheat are her very body, and the cuneiform sign used to indicate her name is precisely such an ear, with all the kernels arranged in perfect order. In Sumerian the name *is* the designated being.

Mesopotamian writing consisted of lines of signs laid out in orderly fashion over clay tablets. The image of the clay surface, worked over methodically, recalls a plowed field. It was logical for Nisaba to also be the goddess of writing. There is nothing unusual about a divinity taking on functions as apparently unrelated as agriculture and writing. In Greece it was held that characters like Palamedes and Musaios were the ones who taught men how to cultivate the land as well as to write all kinds of signs. The Latin nouns *cultus* (crop) and *cultura* (culture) come from the root verb *cultivare* (cultivate), and indicate facts or activities related to working the land, to intellectual knowledge, and to the ability to dominate the world by means of letters, numbers and furrows.

In the dream of Gudea, Nisaba has a specific characteristic. She carries two tablets with her, one with signs on it and the other with lines. Both types of marks were made by a reed or plant stalk, essentially being the wheat stem with an end cut off. The signs are omens of good fortune. It is possible that what is called the "tablet of stars" (*dub mul-an*, Gudea Cylinder A, IV, 26) was a kind of star chart, a written document carrying a promise, or the heavenly plan with a particularly favorable layout for the architectural project proposed. The plan of the temple was inscribed on the lapis lazuli tablet, its deep blue color symbolizing the sky.

Nevertheless, Gudea explains that the plan was not drawn manually by Nisaba (Gudea Cylinder A, VI, 5) but by Nindub, god of copper, a minor deity associated with metalworking. He would thus have acted as an expert draftsman at the orders of Nisaba, the "designer" of the plan together with her brother.

Undoubtedly then, Nisaba was the first goddess-architect in history. She was the deity of agriculture, writing, calculation and architecture. These four tools of divine origin allowed man to control his environment and bring it under control, thus revealing the mysteries of the cosmos. With agriculture, he ordered the earth and inseminated it. Writing made it possible for him to record memories and communicate with supernatural powers. Calculation, together with writing, allowed him to read the signs of codified celestial language. Architecture, finally, was the art that gave man the means to shelter himself, to find refuge.

"City" and "plow tail", in Latin, were nearly homonymous terms, *urbum* and *urvum*. The parallel between architectural and agricultural work, between two ways of planning and ordering a territory, was clear in Roman times. Yet this relationship had already been established in Sumer, as represented by Nisaba. Thanks to the goddess it was possible to make a plan, that is, to attempt to foresee what was going to happen and respond farsightedly.

Architecture is nothing other than one of the many ways man has to relate to the world, to settle the earth and communicate with other powers, whether heavenly or from the underworld. We no longer know if we believe in this function, and have doubts about whether such an architectural art still makes sense.

In the very hymn where Nisaba is praised as *dub-sar mah an-na*, the great scribe of heaven, she is also referred to as *saĝ-tùn*. Following professor Lluís Feliu, this would be translated as "the overseer of surveyors", that is, of those who measure and set out the limits of lands to be farmed or built upon. In this case, the task of land surveying was to lay out the building plan, specifically marking off the lines of the trenches the foundations would be set in. For his part, Jordi Abadal believes that the expression refers more precisely to the idea of a great accountant, where Nisaba would keep close track of all grain crops.

Quite literally, *saĝ* means "chief", and *tùn* refers to a "boundary stone"; it could also refer to a marking line or measuring tape. Thus Nisaba was the overseer of those who laid out bands or strips to set out the limits of the earth. The surveyors were the ones who began architectural projects, laying out the land and marking out the plan of the building to be erected on the ground. This image could be applied to Mesopotamia, where kings like Gudea, renowned for their construction skills, were represented carrying long coils of rope, which would in fact be used to mark out the perimeter of a construction project. Thus Nisaba was the goddess who ruled over the groundbreaking period of the construction process and carried out building tasks. She would make notes with her awl on the tablet, measuring the ground and reworking the layout.

We must recall that Nisaba had a tablet with a star chart on it that she herself had drawn. The drawing could also have been of a celestial plan to be materialized on earth. It would thus be a map of heaven whose lines could be projected down to the plan of a temple, while functioning as a celestial archetype, a "mental image". All Mesopotamian temples had such a celestial referent. In this way Nisaba did indeed operate as a veritable architect, as a designer of dreams, striving to see them become reality.

We are highly indebted to this divinity, mother-goddess and architect-goddess. She was the builder, the one who protected us by laying out limits; she cultivated and nourished us. Nisaba was the wife of Nabu, god of the Babylonian scribes, grandson of Enki. She was an architect, farmer, astrologist and scribe. Her works were read as the future was read, in the growing grain, in the position of the stars, as texts and as buildings are interpreted, both in plans and in reality. Nisaba was the goddess who interpreted the signs gods used to communicate with men. Architectural work, from amongst these signs, would in this way be the expression of divine will.

Straight and Upright

The reed was the stick used for fair measurement in Mesopotamia. The royal scepter was not made of gold; it was a simple plant stalk. This was also the unit of measurement: a straight, flexible plant able to adapt to all circumstances. Thousands of years later Pascal would write that the human being was like a reed: agile, quick and firm, yet always aware, ever-ready.

Reed in Sumerian was *gi*, similar to the Hebrew *qaneh*. The modern noun "cane" thus has very ancient roots. *Kânu* was an Akkadian verb that meant "to build", "to edify", "to create" and "to procreate", and was derived from the Sumerian *gi-na*. This compound word was rooted in *gi*, meaning "to be stable", and referred to the very nature of things that are sure, firm, well-settled and upright. "Upright" in this case was not an adjective solely belonging to the language of geometry, it also referred to an ethical condition.

The Akkadian verb *kânu* was the translation of the Sumerian term *zid*, which picked up on the semantic field already referred to. *Zid* also evoked the idea of rectitude, trust and faith, while furthermore referring to life.

The straight geometric line would thus take on moral values. It was turned into an ethical symbol. What was straight revealed what was upright, both in its condition as an unvarying line and in terms of the values that went along with it: what was straight pointed to the path of virtue.

In Greek *orthos* meant upright and upraised, both in a geometric and moral sense. The orthogonal line, perpendicular to the plan like a plumb line, indicated everything was in its place. In this way each thing fulfilled the aims for which it had been created. The plumb line demonstrates a form has been "well" placed, like a piece of drapery properly hung. To do something "with aplomb" is to be sure of oneself, to have self-confidence. People who are sure of themselves hold their heads up high and their bodies straight; they have nothing to hide. The noun *orthos* is composed of a root, *rt*, that is also found in words like art, rhythm, ritual, articulate and others. All of these terms belong to a semantic field related to the imposition of order. Art (or ritual) has as its objective the composition of the world, its correct construction.

The Indo-European root *rt* is also found in the Greek word *arete*, meaning "merit". It refers to a value associated with behavior, or an exemplary act. Merits are the necessary attributes for things to stand out for being done well. The *arete*, finally, is a virtue that qualifies a way of moving or carrying things, that is, of positioning things in the right place. A virtuoso is still today someone with a developed sense of vocation.

Artistic creation, as related to the creation of forms and of people, has an educating function, and is not unrelated to ethics. Doing something well means neutralizing chaos, deactivating the disorder that goes along with destruction and, ultimately, undoing evil itself.

This is why *gi*, the reed, was a key component in construction. It upheld forms, giving them consistency, articulating them. Its flexibility "comprehended" the nature of things and respected it. The reed symbolized respect towards people and things, the care they should be given, the tenderness each creator should feel for his work. The reed upraised forms and the spirit as well. When the king, who was also judge, appeared reed in hand, people felt secure. The reed symbolized the exercise of justice, that rules for shared living were being established. In turn, certain forms, such as houses and cities, were created where it would be possible to live justly.

The Meaning of Things

Me is one of the most enigmatic terms in the Sumerian language. This is not because we do not know what it means, but quite the contrary: it has many, highly diverse meanings. The term *me* refers to some sixty different things, as oddly disparate as the following: the destruction of cities; prosperity; carpentry technique, intelligence; practical know-how; the place where fertilizer is kept; lies; victory; and forced labor.

For a modern mind there is no way to see any logic at all in such a classification system. It includes objects, actions and values as applied both to the natural world and the heavens, to humans and their creations, but also to the gods.

There are as many translations for the term as specialists taking on the subject of its meaning. An even greater number of articles have been written about it, yet the concept continues to elude. Even so, *me* has an initial translation that is also its simplest: the verb "to be". This is why for some experts, and especially those influenced by Greek metaphysics, *me* referred to the essence of earthly reality. *Me* was found on the earth as well, referring to beings and to the act of being. It could be foundational, though it also indicated the powers enabling the gods to arrange the world.

In looking at the cuneiform sign used to write *me*, we realize it is made up of two short lines set on a right angle, in what resembles the Cross of Saint Andrew. This sign was derived from an archaic symbol, when cuneiform writing was similar to hieroglyphics, composed of drawings and not the abstract marks appearing later with no formal relationship to what they referred to. Yet here the archaic sign shows the same cross. Perhaps it was naturalistic in origin, perhaps representing a staff of authority. At the same time it seems to suggest the spatial coordinates designating the two planes of an architectural drawing, along with the third dimension. In this case *me*, thanks to which the world was conceived, would reveal the concept of order and essence as originally architectural. The *me* that ruled over all successful operations and symbolized their harmonious preparation belonged to the world of spatial arrangement, that is, to urban planning and architecture.

The god Enki arranged the world, creating human beings and organizing a space for them; from then on he was considered the god of craftsmen and above all architects. *Me*, deposited in the god Enki, were the tools making it possible for the world to be "well-composed". Considered plurally then, they were guidelines, the architect's basis for dividing space into lots and arranging it. *Me* were like the structure of space and of all things, the pillars of the world. This conception points to the important role the Sumerians assigned to architecture. Without it, and without the work of the architect (imitating the god Enki's action of putting the universe in order), the world would slip back into chaos. *Me* did not allow beings to lose the place that had been assigned to them, thus becoming the architecture or scaffolding of the world.

This idea would make its way to classical Greece. For Plato, the god of the essences was One, conceived as the great divine power, or just as well the Great Architect. As the god who gave order to the world, he also wielded over what gave meaning and value to those who had settled it.

The Architect's Two Faces

Isimud was both the servant and messenger of Enki. He was readily recognized, as he had two faces on a single head, each looking in the opposite direction. This was why Isimud was also the perfect guardian, as he saw danger coming from anywhere around.

When Enki arranged space with his word, Isimud made it possible. His sole presence traced out (at least virtually) the main horizontal axes that undifferentiated space is made of. Eyes were powerful instruments in Mesopotamia, and Isimud arranged space with a single gaze. In some cases Isimud was even depicted with four faces, each pointing in one of the cardinal directions.

At the gates to Roman cities there was always a god with similar features. Two-faced Janus was never subordinated to any other god, he was the supreme deity. An Etruscan god adopted by the Romans, Janus had no predecessor in Greek mythology, characterized as he was by a double face that looked both to the rising sun and its setting. Janus was the perfect guardian of the weakest parts of any building, the gateways and thresholds. His ability to protect dwellings was not unusual, as he was the Roman god of architecture, and was responsible for the first cities and holy sites. He cared greatly for his creations, protecting them from impending dangers, and his inquisitive double face was always ready to disarm anyone who might try to damage the habitat.

Isimud and Janus were not the only divinities with multiple-faces. We also know of a figure with three faces, personifying youth, maturity and old age respectively, the expression of the virtue of Prudence. It did not control space but time. It ensured the life cycle worked smoothly, passing the values and knowledge of the elderly onto the young, through the inevitable stream of changing roles human beings embody over their lifetimes. Once again, the stability of an eventful life, not only in response to the immensity of space but also to the uncertainty of time, would depend upon a three-faced figure.

In Ancient Greece, Prudence allegorized by a multiple-faced figure was sophrosyne, the highly prized virtue of measure and temperance, privy to the wise. Sophrosyne was related to the capacity to set out limits and define them. According to Plato, it came from "an orderly, harmonious character as seen in control over desire."

The representation of Prudence or Temperance in the Middle Ages emphasized a capacity for order. In its allegorical image a female figure held a compass, a device conceived to put a limit on any sort of excess, whether material or emotional, staving off anything considered perilous for body or mind. The compass was an attribute related to geometry and architecture. It was a tool that helped the architect express his ideas on the map, tracing out the lines shaping the world. It was also an emblem of the supreme gods of creation.

This is why the gods of creation, dominating time and space, were considered to be architects. In contrast to the fragmented perspective of mortal men, the polyhedral vision of architects enabled them to charge the world with body and vigor. They were all eyes, as past, present and future were brought together in a single project. The architect's strength lies in his vision of the world, a spatial capacity giving it substance rather than flattening it out. The architect's wisdom consists in being able to understand the axes of creation.

The Architect and the Weaver

Bašāmu is one of the most common Akkadian verbs referring to creative action. It is usually translated as "to create", and is applied to the production of beings and instruments, amongst which architectural drawings have an important place; the verb also means "to place". Sumerian translated *bašāmu* with the verbal expression *ki...sur*, where *ki* is "earth" and *sur* means "to shape". When referring to property, the expression means "to border", "to set out limits". Yet *sur* had other meanings related to the line running around the exterior of a plot of land: "to demarcate", or "to create an interlocking effect". This would then position us somewhere between architecture and textile production.

The Hebrew verb *banah*, as applied to both human and divine creation, is related to an Akkadian word, *banû*, customarily translated as "to construct". Nevertheless, Hebrew is the only language with a specific verb referring to divine creative action. *Bara'* refers exclusively to action done by Yahweh, whose end will always be the creation of life. Oddly enough, the creation of a "puppet" figure like Eve, who in Genesis was referred to as the wife of Yahweh and not Adam, corresponds to the verb *banah*.

Here though, *bara'* does not mean to create artistically, as the literal translation of the term *bara'* is "to divide" or "to separate from". In this way we can understand the ancient idea of the creative act, conceived as marking out a space for beings or entities that have been separated from primary matter. This recalls Yahweh stirring the Primal Waters there in the beginning, his breath giving them life and whipping them into every imaginable shape.

Bara' was a synonym of *qanah*, which meant both "to earn" and "to create" or "to obtain a good". Equally so, *qanah* was equivalent to the verb *cakak*, meaning "to weave together". The prototype of the woven entity was the human being, defined as a knitted fabric (Psalms 139:13), or as a woven cloth of bones and nerves (Job 10:11).

The art of weaving thus emerges as a truly creative act. As the creator is always an architect, the architect must also be a weaver. The planner's drawing thus becomes a woven fabric of intersecting streets and avenues, a warp and woof grid pattern made of thread.

The word "architecture" is a compound term: *arche*, meaning "principal" (as well as "principle") in Greek, a foundation or origin; and *techne*, habitually translated as "technique". A brief etymological study by Heidegger demonstrates that *techne* is related to the verb *tikto*, with a meaning closer to "to engender" than "to create". Once again, what stands out is the image of the Supreme Creator as an architect. *Techne* is derived from the root *tech*, meaning "to create" or "to give birth". However, this form of creation refers back to the action of the goddesses of fate, pulling life's strings, winding and unwinding them around a spindle. Following on a magnificent Platonic image in the Myth of Er, the idea of the human being as a puppet is here associated with the image of the creator as spinner.

In principle, the family of compound verbs from the root *tech* includes those meaning "to create" and "to procreate". Those referring to manual activities mainly refer to what a carpenter does. As a craftsman responsible for the manufacture and assembly of wooden structures in preparation for a building, the carpenter has to be cleverly skillful in solidly fitting posts and beams together. *Technazo*, quite specifically, means "to knit" or "to weave", and not just metaphorically. The goddess Athena was the patron of carpenters, having passed onto them the required knowledge for working wood, though she was also the protectress of weavers; indeed, she would present herself as the most skilful of them all. Is that not why Arachne competed with Athena (at the expense of the former's life) to find out who was the better weaver and tapestry maker?

Weave, braid and interlock: a carpenter's work and that of a weaver could not be told apart. They labored in the same way, producing solidly worked objects. Yet a carpenter's labor was indistinguishable from an architect's as well, with the architect being the prototype of the creator, able to build spaces where life could be sheltered. The urban fabric was his work.

The supreme deity had similar talents as the weaving goddesses of Luck, Necessity and Fortune. These goddesses protected the cities, because as weavers they were also the ones who armed them. Fortune, with her head crowned with a wall, was more specifically the protecting goddess of urban space. Fortune hangs by a thread, with the architect pulling the strings. Or perhaps he is the one entangling them.

Foundations

The walls and part of the city of Babylon were rebuilt by order of Saddam Hussein in the 1980s and 1990s. These new walls were paper thin, and are little more than a theatrical set, simple dividers serving as the support for reproductions of ancient reliefs featuring guardian animals, with glazed lions, bulls and dragons. These figures can only be seen properly face on, as from the side the profile of the reliefs is too flat to be at all intelligible.

This is the image of Babylon that has seen the light, the one that has been given play in the media. As you walk up to visit the city, the path leading to the artificial set at one point becomes very steep, and the ground seems to fall off on one side towards a valley bottom. From out of the depths of this valley another set of walls are seen to rise, the high points of their ramparts at the same level of the path. It quickly becomes clear that these walls are different: they mark off a wide ceremonial access way some one hundred yards long. In contrast to the newer walls, these fortifications are immensely thick. They look like heavy blocks of rock the valley waters have opened a deep gorge through. Yet the hefty profile of these other walls is no mirage. We are speaking of the original walls, erected some 2600 years ago, the "authentic" walls of Babylon.

Why then do they seem to have sunk? Is it possible that the level of Babylon in the seventh century BC was over thirty yards lower than now?

The answer is that the walls of that time had been completely destroyed; the Neo-Assyrians did not leave a single stone standing. The last Neo-Babylonian kings, however, made the decision to raise the city of the god Marduk once more, some time before it would definitively fall to the Persians. For a period of time Babylon continued to surprise travelers come to visit from the known world.

In Mesopotamia it was not possible to build on virgin land, unless for some reason the buildable land had been sullied. The requirement was that all new construction had to be done over the top of a previous building site. This is why the monarchs made such a great effort to send out their builders in search of the layouts of previously existing temples and palaces buried beneath the ground, before ordering new projects to be undertaken.

The Neo-Babylonian kings were left with a serious predicament: the outlines of the ancient walls had disappeared, and there was no way to know where they had been. The reconstruction of such structures could not therefore be carried out according to tradition, and no king would have risked making a mockery of the gods, heeding the priests' diligent warnings.

This made it essential to find a way to uncover these urban outlines and rediscover the past. Only when such information was clearly at hand would a king order the entire fortress to be built, though while taking extreme care in doing so. The glazed bricks used for the animal reliefs were set into the walls in carefully chosen pairs, so as to create the effect of long rows of fierce creatures watching over the city. The walls of the rebuilt city of Babylon were protected by neatly aligned rows of menacing lions, uneasy bulls and dragons resembling unicorns, running from the base up to the highest battlements.

Then, once they had been built, the walls were buried once more. Carefully positioned below the earth, they were interred to make it possible for them to be discovered once more. The same walls that later on would impress Herodotus or whoever was advising him would be raised over top of these earlier ones. Babylon had once more become a signal fire, shining its light out unto the world.

A few millennia ago these later walls were gone, torn down by the Persians, demolished by the troops of Alexander as well. What we now come across, much to our surprise, are not the walls that had been raised beside the Euphrates River (in spite of the fact that the Euphrates crossed through the city and past its fortress and the area reserved for sacred rituals as well), but the ones that had been buried beneath them. Hidden there, they have avoided being the object of either ire or indifference, now huddled in the depths of a hollow.

The Depths

In the Sumerian city of Uruk we find Giparu, one of the most ancient temples in history. Like the walls of Babylon, it was built to be later buried, so that over top of it they could erect a temple we have no evidence of at all.

Gaston Bachelard did not like living in a Parisian apartment. He detested those unenchanted "concrete boxes" grounding all flights of the imagination. His disapproval of urban dwellings was not based on their being too modern, but on their incapacity to be anything close to what a house should be. Bachelard thought that one's living quarters should be a confluence of verticality, uniting the sky, represented by the attic, with the infernal confines of the basement.

Bachelard felt that a house should be a place able to link light and darkness, reaching up as high as possible without forgetting its roots in the domain of the dead. This would mean both fear and hope would be activated, as the residence would be imaginarily inhabited by angels and ghosts. The basement has the task of darkly reproducing the structure of the home, being its sinister though necessary pole of contrast, for in a home all space is shared by the living and the dead. This is what creates the conditions for a space of lasting rest.

This idea of architecture is quite similar to what the Mesopotamians applied to their own houses, conceiving them as divine dwellings. Temples for their part tended to be built over top of preexisting structures. When these latter were no longer standing, after having disappeared, or when the choice had been made to build on virgin land, a previous construction was buried on the site, so as to serve as the foundation of what would then be erected for all to see.

Such buried temples tended to be dedicated to the powers of the underworld, though we are not referring necessarily to infernal gods. They could just as well have been ancestral ones, bound to primary elements such as water and earth, and to the first little mound of land the luminous gods would be upraised on.

These earlier deities were accustomed to the night. The way to get a temple to shine was to call on the night's powers, so as to illuminate the dwelling places of the heavenly gods. Such underground temples, like crypts, were more important than visible ones, as they united the powers that had brought life into the universe. They worked as depositories, enclosures of dreams. A true temple was thus a dark space reaching down into the depths of mother earth.

An echo of such beliefs made its way to Greece, and even to Christianity. The Temple of Apollo in Delphos was constructed over top of a previous holy site, perhaps a cave or a chasm, dedicated to the goddess Gaea, the earth mother.

It was inconceivable that a temple without these buried areas beneath it could hold up. It would have lacked the precise characteristics that give a temple meaning: its connection to the powers comprising the world, for whom life and death (and always in that order) were inevitable steps along the way.

Apollo and the Bible

The builder gods blandished sharpened weaponry as they marked out plans on paper, tablets or the earth itself. A single awl was enough, as long as the surface could be clearly cut. Yet the gods are cruel as well. They construct, but they can also send their creations back to a state of original chaos, and do so without warning, whether in a fit of rage or on the basis of a cool-headed decision.

In Greece, the god of architecture Apollo always carried a long knife. This allowed him to cut his way through the forest, marking out paths that would endure. It also helped him to open up clearings in the woods, removing the brush to found cities or holy sites. Apollo had no mercy, slashing away without remorse. Nature would never sprout up again in the lands he had passed through. The paths he cleared ended up uniting cities, making communication lines easier. Thanks to such paths, human beings no longer had to risk getting lost in the dense undergrowth. The forests would no longer stop them from knowing where they were going.

This image of an armed Apollo wiping out any outgrowth that might debilitate the communication network, and with it the structures set into it, does not coincide with what his image had been over a long period of time. The lyre and not the dagger had been taken to be his favorite attribute, for Apollo was the enchanting god of music. This was true, but he was also a divinity who handled a blade better than anyone else when it came to slicing space into pieces.

This view of a criminal Apollo (which is the one the Greeks had) endured throughout antiquity and found its echo in the Book of Revelation. The presence of a Greek divinity in the Biblical text could be surprising, but the image we have of him there is in line with the god's true character.

Sitting on high upon his throne, God held up a scroll, sealed with seven seals. Each one of them contained an important detail regarding what was to come. No one was able to break the seals, except for a lamb covered with seven eyes, representing the seven breaths of God.

When the scroll was opened, the seven messengers of God sounded their trumpets. With every new blast, a cataclysm befell them. The sun closed down like a giant eye, never to be seen again. When the fifth trumpet sounded, a star fell and God gave the key to the shaft of the bottomless pit to the fifth messenger, who threw open the depths of chaos. The Greek term referring to this place (Revelation 9:2) is *abyssos*, synonym of *chasma*, a term related to *chaos*.

As soon as the abyss was opened, a dark line of smoke rose up from the depths, covering the sky in darkness. Then locusts came out of the smoke, as powerful as scorpions. Insects were seen that were similar to armored horses, making a noise like that of chariots:

> They had as king over them the angel of the Abyss, whose name in Hebrew is Abaddon and in Greek is Apollyon. [*Habent super se regem angelum abyssi, cui nomen Hebraice Abaddon et Graece nomen habet Apollyon.*]
> Revelation 9:11 (The New Vulgate Bible)

This description of the domains of Apollo corresponds to the Greek tradition. Apollo reigned in the Temple of Delphos, connected by a deep pit to the *chasma*, the underworld, from which intoxicating vapors rose. We might ask whether the association between the locust and Apollo was based on the resemblance between this insect and the cicada, a creature dedicated to him.

The infernal character of Apollo was a true reflection of the contrasting sentiments this god provoked amongst the Greeks. It was true he was a builder, but to build he had previously seen fit to raze the earth, erasing its impurities and returning it to its original state of chaos—only then to shape it anew.

The Tablets of the Law

The image of an enraged Charlton Heston (or Moses we should say) raising the long tablets of the law above his head, poised to smash them upon the ground, is unforgettable. As in the Cecil B. DeMille movie, for our collective imagination stone tablets with short horizontal lines on them (as if a poem in verse) could only mean the Ten Commandments.

Nevertheless, the biblical text does not quite say this. What it describes is perhaps less impressive, though much more in line with Ancient Middle Eastern tradition, within which the Old Testament should be considered.

We are referring to the scene (Exodus 35:11) where Moses descends from Mount Sinai the final time, after having previously inscribed a copy of the first tablets. It was that first set he would end up smashing to pieces when seeing how the Israelites, feeling forsaken, had cast a statue of a Golden Calf to worship. After this well-known episode, Moses ordered his people to repent and literally obey what was written on stone.

The tablets did not contain moral edicts or lay out rules of behavior. Rather, they called on the Israelites to build something: a *mishkan*. This Hebrew term is usually translated as "tabernacle", though it really means "residence" or "dwelling". The modern translation comes from the Latin Vulgate Bible. The word *tabernaculum* specifically comes from the Greek and not the Hebrew version of the text, where *mishkan* is translated as *skene*. *Skene* was the word used to refer to a theatre set, an ephemeral construction set upon a stage that could have had wheels to make it portable. *Skene* also could mean "hut", referring to both a modest home construction and a temporary structure like a tent, its roof held up by four poles.

In this way then, the tablets contained the graphic and written instructions for designing and constructing an ephemeral, even transhumant dwelling place for Yahweh. It would be a small shelter carrying items for cult worship: the Ark of the Covenant.

The texts in Hebrew, Greek and Latin are clear: the tablets contained an architectural project. Yahweh shows Moses:

The pattern of the tabernacle and the pattern of all its furniture.
Exodus 25: 8

The original Hebrew uses the noun *tabnīt*, meaning "imprint", though also "model". The Greek text employs the term *paradeigma*, "model". The Vulgate version in turn uses *similitudo*, that is, "image". What Yahweh was ordering Moses to write and draw on the tablets was the floor plan and perspective.

The details given in the Biblical account are quite thorough, clearly explaining the measurements and materials to be used to build this portable temple, including the layout and how it should be decorated. The Biblical description includes the priestly vestments, its curtains, perfumes, the coffers and the candelabrum. Yahweh speaks like someone with unfathomable knowledge of craft technique, meticulously setting out the details of the fabric to be used to make clothing and drapery, like an expert tailor.

The ark is defined as a miniature temple, comprised of the same number of sections the future Temple in Jerusalem would have much later on.

In his concern to properly execute the plans and construction work, Yahweh chooses a skilled artisan who is bestowed with divine clairvoyance. Bezalel, son of Uri, son of Hur, of the tribe of Judah (Exodus 31:1-2), is granted *hokmah*, referring both to a craftsperson's manual skill and the intelligence of someone attuned to the arts. He is given *sophia* and *episteme*, wisdom and discernment in the Greek version, which in the Vulgate is given as *sapientia, et intelligentia et scientia in omni opere*. This gift is the spirit of God anointing Bezalel, inspiring him. Though still an expert craftsman while building the Ark, he takes on the condition of someone "inspired". God infuses him with his gift, and so, in a certain way, participates in the construction work. Bezalel becomes the architect of the Ark because he has risen to "the level" of the Architect of the world, having delved deeply into his secrets. Bezalel's creative capacity is seen in his very name, which means "in His shadow".

The choice of Bezalel is obvious: he is a carpenter. In antiquity carpenters were seen as shamans, able to transform the power of trees into the service of craft creation. Trees held up the celestial vault, and kept the three cosmic levels together in united and orderly fashion (hell, earth and the sky, connected by the roots, the trunk and the branches).

A carpenter, like a smith or a potter, played with the powers of the Earth. That is why he produced animate works, able to guard what they held within. As a carpenter Bezalel prefigured Christ while overshadowing Yahweh. It is perhaps for this reason that Christianity downplayed the character, while the Freemasons would revive it once more.

The true content of the tablets and the relationship Yahweh establishes with Moses and Bezalel is repeated years later when the project for the Temple in Jerusalem is completed. Once again, Yahweh delivers David the visual and written documents needed to design and build the Temple, though in this case the commission to build it would be given to Hiram.

This manner of working belongs to the Mesopotamian tradition, whereby the gods encouraged kingly action, speaking to them in dreams about what they had to do once awake, providing them with all the information required to correctly carry out any project.

Bezalel and later Hiram were exemplary architects, able to create first with words. The world is found in stories, and those who deploy words build parallel worlds more reliable than reality itself, worlds it is sometimes necessary to find refuge in. Stone construction came later on. The Ark, the dwelling place of Yahweh, is presented as a miniaturized image of the universe.

Architecture was too important an art to be left in the hands of mortals with no divine inspiration.

THE HOUSE

Vessel and Home

For a long period of time it was thought that agriculture, animal husbandry and human settlement were associated cultural phenomena. They were held to represent the step from the Paleolithic to the Neolithic, which took place around 9000 BC in the long, narrow strip known as the Fertile Crescent. Human beings settled there, leaving the hunting and gathering practices they had survived on for tens of thousands of years. Hunting and gathering was replaced by the production of grain, botanical fibers like linen and leguminous plants, with the surpluses kept in silos built on the outer limits of any settlement. The only doubt experts had was related to the order these three activities took place: did human beings settle so as to later cultivate lands and domesticate animals? Or was it the combination of agriculture and herding that led them to leave their nomadic lives and settle down for good?

Here too, however, reality is more complex than theory. Villages from about twelve thousand years ago have been found with data suggesting the inhabitants were fully settled while remaining hunter-gatherers. There are a few other sites with evidence of cultivated lands and herding, though the people were not settled into villages at all. In these latter cases the humans worked in arduous tasks in agriculture and with livestock, but continued to lead nomadic lives.

For all this, nine thousand years ago villages appeared in great numbers throughout the Middle East, in Palestine, Syria, northern Iraq and Anatolia. Furthermore, a new kind of object was found in the ruins of these sites: pottery.

Pottery arose some ten thousand years ago, though it would take a thousand more years for its presence to become widespread. Whether an accidental factor or not, the increasingly urban character of the region coincided with mass pottery production, which was still not being done on a wheel.

Pots and jars were used to keep foodstuffs, and it is also possible they were used as vessels for the "kitchen". At the same time, it could be that their main function was less utilitarian than symbolic. A quite common use for larger ceramic jars was as funerary urns, with the remains of the deceased placed inside; this meant the size of such objects could vary greatly. The dead person thus made his home in a jar, his final dwelling place. It was an enclosed space, well defined by a narrow neck or a wooden lid on top, protecting the ancestor's remains. In some cases these urns (found in great quantities over the region) would take on the shape of a house or an animal.

So as to assist the "ancestors" in the task of protecting their descendants, funerary urns were stored in the home or quite frequently buried beneath it. In this way a house was built as if it had sprouted up from one of these vessels, here turned into the fount of a sheltering space. They were models, in a quite literal sense, which people's homes were built from.

The first spaces to be built had circular floor plans, with the foundations set into the ground. They were quite possibly inspired by the shape of the funerary urn itself, those "homes for the dead" that had been molded in clay and fired. It is also possible that the shape of the urns drew inspiration from the primordial shape of a womb, or from the rounded caves where certain animals spent the winter.

It is quite likely that the living sought a dwelling place similar to what was granted to the dead. Partially-buried homes and cabins were like giant vessels. We might recall that in Archaic Greece (thousands of years later) oversized recipients were placed over top of tombs as funerary steles; these objects could reach up to six feet high, as large as small huts. They were even taller than the statues of most Greek heroes.

The home would in this way be a vessel, a place of refuge, like when we bring our hands together to hold water when offering a small child something to drink, or like when we protect our faces from danger: a precautionary, concave space. Perhaps after this the recipients began to be used for food, though whatever the case, in a certain sense their function was beneficial to life. They were used to feed the hungry and quench thirst. They were like a last hope, a final refuge of hospitality. They were receptacles of life, like houses, like final resting places. In this way, therefore, the house could be seen as the most fragile of all containers.

Guardians of the Home

Dogs were quite likely the first domesticated animals, as they were used to guide the flocks and keep watch over the home. In Mesopotamia they were emblematic animals, along with bulls, lions, eagles and the carp. The dog was associated with the goddess Gula, and while hybrid depictions of gods were not customary in Mesopotamia, upon occasion she was given a canine head.

Gula was a principal deity; she was quite likely the most important goddess in the Mesopotamian pantheon, together with Inanna. In spite of this she never had a clear equivalent in Greco-Latin mythology, where the dog's role was exclusively in funerary rites and magic, and dogs were associated with Hecate, the goddess of sorcery. This relationship between the dog and the realm of the dead, present in Egypt as well, was common in Mesopotamia, though it could not be said to be a unique or essential feature.

As the daughter of An, Gula was the consort of Ninurta, the liberating warrior god who took on the heavenly dragon and whose blood fertilized the cosmos—a mythical character recalling Saint George. The goddess had various names that personified her various functions. Gula was the one who brought healing water. The constellation Aquarius was her sign in the firmament, making the rivers flow more strongly when its stars shone most brightly in the night sky. Upon occasion Gula was also known as Nanshe, goddess of agriculture, land division and writing, a goddess who regulated life in order to ensure it thrived. In various hymns she was invoked as the goddess of medicine, protecting and healing the ill. She knew how to draw clear lines between order and disorder, and for this reason was also extolled as the goddess of limits. She kept with her the tools required to measure space—rope and measuring sticks—as told in the Gula Hymn, written by Bullutsa-rabi.

This relationship between space and the healing function made Gula the protectress of spaces along with any sort of life found in them. She was the goddess who above all watched over enclosed spaces, and this is why Gula was the guardian of domestic space. She reigned in intimate spaces, which prospered thanks to the material objects (the "abundance") that Gula brought to them. Dogs were the guardians called upon to watch over the places dedicated to her.

The relationship between architecture and medicine has been observed in Egypt, Greece and Rome as well. The Egyptian god of architecture, Ptah, had his equivalent in the Ptolemaic period in Asclepius, son of Apollo, the Greek god of medicine and architecture. This association between two types of prevention, one spatial, the other medical, was found in Mesopotamia with Gula, the goddess who took on the double task of caring for both homes and those who were ill.

As the hymns proclaim, Gula was the great goddess, the mother of all humans. Perhaps it is time to call out to her once more.

The Maternal Home

La Sumerian writing was pictographic in the early period. Natural drawings worked to denominate recognizable things. Complex concepts were hard to express, which was why they had to fall back on word combinations, adding non-representational signs to them, so as to point to their function. In this way, for example, the union of the words "leg" and "path" with "arrow" was read as "walk".

Something similar took place with abstract concepts. As painters can well attest, there is a need to come up with a set of naturalistic figures to represent an abstract idea. In this way "liberty", for Delacroix, was a full-bosomed young woman, one breast bared, brandishing a weather-worn flag over a heap of ruins.

Sumerian culture was founded on a sharply hierarchical theocratic society where supernatural powers conditioned life on earth. In spite of everything, it does seem they had some idea of freedom, or at least they had a set of graphic signs that are customarily translated as such: *ama-ar-gi$_4$*.

Ama is a sign that appears in the early period of writing. It was a geometric shape with a star-shaped sign inside of a square, crowned in turn by a triangle. The image was not at all difficult to read: the sign represented a constructed house with a peaked roof, similar to the kind children draw. The star was the only feature that could give rise to certain interpretational doubts.

This sign also meant "mother", and here the sound of the word *ama* will be familiar to us. The maternal home symbolized the values brought to the fore by both the house and the mother. The sign also happened to mean "warmth" and "maternal womb". That is, it referred to an inviting interior space charged with life, or an empty space teeming with possibilities. The sign always referred to an interior hideaway where you could rest, and this explains the decisive subtlety the star suggests. Besides this, it was a feminine space, as *ama* is also translated as "gynaeceum".

The word *gi$_4$* was written with a recognizable image, though interpreting it nowadays might be a challenge. The sign shows a plant where the spiked stalk leans sharply to the side. The sign is not showing a plant laid low by the wind; rather, it is a stalk that has been bent by the weight of the grain. This sign is not read as "stalk", "spike" or "plant", which are usually represented by similar signs. Rather, it designates a verb: "to return", "to go back", "to regress". The fallen stalk is pointing in a certain direction.

Ar or *r* are case endings of the dative case, indicating where an action is going. In this way, then, *ama-ar-gi$_4$* literally means to return to the mother or the maternal home.

Freedom, then, meant going back to the original space, to the mother's womb. *Ama-ar-gi$_4$* is now translated as "freedom". Even so, this may not be the exact meaning, as it is a word that is ineludibly marked by connotations that cannot easily be applied to a society of the fourth millennium BC. In fact, the set of signs *ama-ar-gi$_4$* should be rendered as "liberation" or "restitution". Or, to be even more exact, as "return to origin".

What we understand by freedom would have been for the Sumerians both a breaking of bonds, whether material, social or religious, and the return to a paradisiacal state that had only existed at life's advent. Unlike in the Delacroix painting, or in Judeo-Christian culture more generally, freedom does not involve advancing towards a utopian future. Rather, it denotes a movement in regression towards a starting point, to the mother's warm and tender arms, where the human being feels protected and can act without care. It is a place where no one is obliged to do anything, and where everything is possible.

The maternal home, which in nineteenth century literature is an oppressive, unsettling space, was conceived six thousand years ago as an ideal space, an interior domain requiring all chains to be thrown off at the threshold.

House and Shadow

The first house and the first city were built after a period when human beings had lived harmoniously together (getting along with animals and gods
as well). In Paradise, Eden, Neverland (like the Peruvian *Jauja*) or Primal
Earth, human beings had no enemies. They had no need to hide from each
other or be concerned about how to defend themselves. The few settled
areas, according to Ovid (*Metamorphoses*, Book I: 96) had no moats; as Virgil
mused (*Eclogues* IV: 33-34), cities had no gates and no walls.

Supernatural powers, pleased with the creatures of their making, did not
let calamities constantly befall them, protecting them from any evil that
might incite their mistrust. In Paradise humans lived in the open air, and
there was no need for clothing. Textiles and roofs were unnecessary, since
there was no such thing as mistrust. Everything was equally available to
everyone, there was no reason for the most valued fruits to be hidden away.

Brother killing brother tainted the peace. In almost all cultures, conflict
arose between twin siblings, held to be the prototypes and fathers of humanity. As soon as the first crime had been committed, humans had to hide
from themselves and from the gazes of others, ashamed of their doings and
fearful of those who had been harmed. The overall mood soured, guilt took
hold, and with it an unavoidable need to hide.

In the Bible, after Cain murders his brother Abel, Yahweh expels him
from the Garden of Eden, condemning him to a life of wandering, denying
him any possibility of settling down and resting. Nevertheless, at the very
last moment he is allowed to create a space where all those who have been
banished like him might find respite. This was the first city, christened
with the name of Cain's first born: Enoch.

This city was then the antithesis of Paradise. It was a place surrounded
by walls with only a few main gates, always kept shut and heavily defended.
Each inhabitant was given a dwelling place, with heavy walls creating
sharp divisions between each home; from then on these people have lived
inside their four walls. The only way to survive was to live within such an
enclosure and hold out until death, no matter how many years it might take:
this was the destiny of man.

The origin of architecture (of the city, of human habitat) is linked to the first crime, the first sacrifice. It implies the insertion of walls and a roof between man and god, thus darkening inhabited space.

House, cell, chapel—in Romance languages, evolved from Latin, terms like these have a similar etymology (in Spanish: *casa, celda, capilla*), as they are spaces that were created at the same time with the same function: to hide humans from any degree of excess light that could make their miseries known to others.

Cain, as Victor Hugo tells us, sought in vain to hide himself from the accusatory gaze of God. He created spaces for himself that were ever more recondite and secluded, ending up with no choice but to curl himself up inside a tomb. Yet even then, though surrounded by heavy stone on all sides, the penetrating eye of God remained watchful and insistent:

> Then added: "I will live beneath the earth,
> As a lone man within his sepulchre.
> I will see nothing; will be seen of none."
> They digged a trench, and Cain said: "'Tis enow,"
> As he went down alone into the vault;
> But when he sat, so ghost-like, in his chair,
> And they had closed the dungeon o'er his head,
> The Eye was in the tomb and fixed on Cain.
>
> Victor Hugo, "Cain", *La légende des siècles*.
> [Translated into English and published by *Dublin University Magazine*, vol. LV, no. CCCXXVI, February 1860, pp. 223-224].

This balsamic shade is thus what gives meaning to architecture, understood here as shelter and not in terms of the spectacle of monumentality. Humans would not have survived if they had been exposed to the sun in those latitudes; nor would they have been able to withstand the stares of others. Perhaps the day will come—however illusory this might seem—when humans will once again choose to live without roofs over their heads, just as in the beginning of time.

House and Night

The first book of the Bible begins with the Hebrew word *bereshit*, which in general terms means "once upon a time", "one day" or "in the beginning". The first letter of the Bible thus corresponds to the consonant "b", a letter called *bet*, which also means "house". This would give rise to Cabbalistic biblical exegesis, as initiated by Moses de León in the thirteenth century, where the creative act of Yahweh was interpreted as an architectural gesture. In consequence, Paradise would be comparable to a house.

In Akkadian, "house" was said *bītu* or *bētānu*, which is where we derive the root of the Hebrew *bet* and the Arabic *bayt*. *Bītu*, however, was related to the verb *bītānû*, translated as "to spend the night". The house is then the place where humans and animals find shelter in the night. This relationship between *bītu* and *bītānû*, and their inevitable contrast to the outdoor world, points to the house as the place where fire is lit. It is a space that is not clearly distinguishable by day, but which by night becomes a point of light, announcing its vocation as a *locus* of hospitality. The house is the shelter that allows us to rest without worry, it offers a degree of security that means we can lower our guard, close our eyes and dream of other things. In the same way, all weapons are barred from this domestic space, they are kept somewhere else. What is distinct about *bītu* is its condition as *bītānû*, that is, as an interior space. It is a space that is secluded and defensible, where any wanderer by day can confidently settle in to spend the night. Excepting those whose task is to guard the house, no one spends the night on duty. The relationship between the house and the tomb is found precisely in the idea that both of them are places of rest, whether for a single night or for eternity.

Bītu has the same root as the Akkadian preposition *bit*, a word used for both time and space functions. It can just as well mean "where" as "when", and allows the speaker to situate something or someone in a given place and time. It provides us with the coordinates required to avoid getting lost. The here and now that *bit* denotes is a house: a secluded space where it is possible to put down roots. Any concrete point in empty or open space can only be conceived as an interior. The house is therefore the reference point that positions us in space. It helps keep us from getting lost, from becoming errant or suffering souls. The house fixes our place and allows us to hide ourselves away, physically and mentally, since once inside we no longer have any need to be watchful, unsettled or afraid.

The House of God

At the end of the nineteenth century academics dedicated to the earliest archeological studies of the Middle East used the Bible as a valid source for their research. The Bible tells us about the city of Ur, Abraham's birthplace, though it says nothing of Sumerian culture. It was a time when digs had begun on the largest Sumerian cities: Ur, Uruk, Eridu and Lagash. Tablets with unintelligible writing on them were unearthed, not to be deciphered with any precision until century's end. In this way, slowly but surely, a civilization that until then had been completely forgotten was unearthed: Sumer.

Work on the digs uncovered massive architectural structures from ancient times, taking us as far back as the fourth millennium BC. Some buildings' circular floor plans were soon interpreted as denoting temples. Temples and more temples rose out of the desert sand. It would come to be said that Sumerian cities were dominated by innumerable sacred spaces. In this regard, Jean-Louis Huot argues that the early image of the Sumerian city-state was derived from the model of the Vatican papal state, whose society, downtrodden by an omnipresent and dictatorial priestly class, was similar to Victorian England. Sumerian cities were thus given an image that sharply contrasted with Greek civil society, making it possible to mark out the difference between a philosophical, free-thinking West and an East given over to the supernatural.

The great number of hymns dedicated to temples from the end of the second millennium would seem to corroborate this image of Sumer as a land of inclement priests and sacred cities, held firmly under the imperial thumb of so many religious sites. Temples, did we say? The words we have for them are the Sumerian *é* and the Akkadian *bītum*. *Bet* and *bayt* are also the name of a consonant, the letter "b", written by a sign of a three-sided square, with the vertical left line missing. This sign recalls the floor plan of a modest building, of a house. It is no accident. The Sumerian *é* and the Semitic terms *bītum*, *bet* and *bayt* mean "house", as simple as that may be.

Nowadays the majority of these large structures excavated in the nineteenth century are interpreted as community spaces rather than temples per se. In any case, we know that the gods did not have temples, but homes.

Their homes were larger and more luxurious than human residences, but were homes just the same. The gods lived in dwelling places that were similar to what the Arabs would live in later on, looking onto interior spaces with their backs turned to the street. Their spaces were reserved for a few guests, for priests and monarchs, though in no case were they substantially different from human residences.

It has come as somewhat of a surprise that Ancient Greece had no term to refer to temples. Unlike what was seen in Mesopotamia, in Greece the buildings consecrated to the gods gave no cause for argument. The texts refer to the existence of *oikoi* or *domoi*. When Apollo, in the Homeric epic, builds his Temple at Delphos, the term used is *oikoi*. Both *oikoi* and *domos*, giving rise to the Latin term *domus* (which is where we get the adjective "domestic"), mean "house". If we look at a Greek temple carefully, it is clear it is nothing more than a parallelepiped with a peaked roof, a conventional house. The temple is the exclusive dwelling place of the deity, there attended to by his servants the priests.

The Greek term *temenos*, the Latin *templum* (where our term "temple" comes from) and the Sumerian *temen* are all derived from a now-forgotten Indo-European term referring to enclosed space. More specifically, it refers to a private space with restricted access. These terms set out the private character of divine space, understood as an impregnable reserve where the god was the true lord of his abode.

This concept of the temple would be turned around by monotheist religions like Christianity and Islam. While still upholding the domestic nature of such spaces, an *ekklesia* is a community. The church is the house of the people there congregated to carry out certain actions, like prayer. In this case, unlike what we see in Egypt, Mesopotamia, Greece and Rome, the divinity does not live in his house, and rarely even drops by. The statues and paintings there found are not the body of the god, but simply images, rememorating his time on earth. The heavenly powers do not dwell in the church, as it is not their house but the house of the faithful. Christ had already claimed he would build *his* church with the bodies of each and every one of his believers.

Islam accentuated the strictly profane character of the "temple". The mosque is derived from Mohammed's house in Medina, where he would host friends and acquaintances, speaking or sharing his visions with them. A mosque is a community center where you eat, play, talk, trade, study and pray. At the same time, it is perfectly integrated into the urban structure. In a certain sense, it symbolizes the city itself, in turn represented by this assembly space, the house of us all. In contrast, pagan temples were barred to human beings. The gods, playing the role of dourly possessive proprietors, only let certain carefully-chosen people into their confines. The pagan gods were never welcoming hosts; glowing bright in their own splendor, they had no need to show the least bit of consideration towards any dark and shadowy human presence.

The gods are a great human invention. The temples should thus be understood as the reflection of the image we have of our own conception of domestic space, whether open or closed, in function of our relationships with relatives and neighbors. The gods are all too human, and behave as such. When locked tightly inside their houses, not a soul—not from heaven, not from earth—can get inside.

The House of the Rising Sun

Sumer could seem to us to be the cradle of civilization, though the Sumerians did not consider themselves to be first. They claimed they came from a more ancient and perfect world, namely Dilmun. Their most precious materials came from there, including wood and copper. Dilmun was their El Dorado, described in the Sumerian myths as the Promised Land.

Ziusudra, also known as Utnapishtim, was the sole survivor of the Flood, together with his family. He owed his salvation to the Ark, which enabled him to resist the raging rains and seas, counseled by the god of the waters, Enki. It is thanks to him that humanity was able to overcome the cataclysm, and for this reason he was granted eternal life in Dilmun.

It would seem that Dilmun consisted of a peninsula and a group of islands, like present-day Bahrain, though it could also have been as far away as Saudi Arabia. In 1954 a Danish archeological mission unearthed the most perfectly conceived Mesopotamian holy site in this region. We refer to the Barbar Temple (or temples), a building made up of three overlaid holy sites built one over the other over a period of a thousand years. The first of these was from around the year 3000 BC, while the following two were built on the ruins of the first, most likely between 2200 and 1700 BC. These temples have a Sumerian typology, with a series of rectangular platforms set over top of a larger oval mound. The temple itself has a number of chapels where altars and ceramic offerings have been found.

The Barbar temples are the best preserved Sumerian religiou₃ buildings. While in Mesopotamia all construction was done in adobe bricks, leading to gradual deterioration from strong rains and the effects of ground water, the Barbar temples were done with perfectly cut and fitted stone blocks whose state of conservation is still admirable.

It is quite possible that this holy site was dedicated to the god Enki, or more precisely to his *paredra* (or sacred consort), the goddess Ninhursag; in Dilmun she was also known as Ninsikila. Enki was the god of fresh water, and his wife was at the same time his mother and the mother-goddess, associated with the heights and the depths.

At the base of the temple a stairway goes down into the earth, turning into a vaulted passageway leading to a well full of water, fed by some sort of natural, subterranean source. Perhaps this well was Abzu, the mythical space that was the goddess of the waters, wisdom and a foundational spring all at once.

The current name in Arabic, Barbar, would come from the Sumerian *é-babbar*, where *babbar* or *bar-bar* is "white" or "bright", and *babbar-é* refers to the land where the sun rises: the White (*babbar*) House (*é*), or the House of the Rising Sun. For the Sumerians, the sun rose from out of the Primal Waters; indeed, it was born in Dilmun.

All Sumerian holy places had a replicate of Abzu, whether a well or a pond, symbol of the life the site was meant to guarantee. Yet the holy temple of Barbar was found in the first land, where death held no sway. The waters enclosing the temple, and upon which it was placed, were the very waters that had given birth to the world. It could be that the Barbar temple was considered to be the origin of life.

The Barbar temple also controlled trade from the Indus Valley to the Tigris and Euphrates Delta. It was a veritable source of life in both a physical and spiritual sense. Mesopotamia was intimately bound to this temple, and its life depended upon it. It is no coincidence that the denouement of Sumerian culture at the beginning of the second millennium BC would coincide with the period this temple was abandoned.

Matriarchal Temples

Unlike what is found in Greece, Rome or India, in Mesopotamia (and more specifically in Sumer) there were no architectural or construction treatises dictating the most appropriate forms or typologies to be used for certain buildings. We have evidence of hymns written to temples, though they do not speak of formal features, and while there are a number of descriptions of holy sites, they do not lay out a set of formal rules that had to be respected.

We do know that temples found in cities, unlike those outside of them, were usually surrounded by a wall and had other rooms and storehouses. The temple itself would be built around a central rectangular space—a courtyard—that could be covered; this in turn was lined with other spaces and chapels. While it is not clear if that is how things always were, it does seem that the temples did not respond to a specific architectural typology. Not even the size of the building was particularly meaningful. We often have doubts when interpreting archeological remains, to the extreme that in a place like Lagash we do not know if we are dealing with a palace, a religious site or (however odd it may seem) a bridge.

There are three temples that are particularly different from the typology we have already referred to. The Oval Temple of Khafajah, the well-known temple of Ninhursag at Tell al-'Ubaid and the temple of Inanna in Lagash share features that are unique in the world. In certain epochs the sanctuary inside these temples had a divine dwelling place set on a high podium, along with other rooms, and a wall or double ring of walls set on an oval floor plan surrounding the respective building. These temples were separated from the city street structure, and were placed apart, on their own, poorly connected to the rest of the urban layout, if related at all. In all cases the city grew around them, though the interstitial spaces were never filled in. The holy site did not fit in with the city, it was like a foreign entity. Or perhaps we should say that it was the city that did not match the temple, as if confronting two opposing concepts.

A three-temple sample is no doubt a bit thin if what we want to do is define the typology of a building. We know that two of these holy sites were the dwelling places of feminine divinities, while the god the Oval Temple was consecrated to is not known. The Oval Temple was built over a plot of land that had previously been occupied by housing. These buildings from before had been razed, the ground cleared, the foundations wiped away, with the ground then covered by a thick layer of fresh earth, so that the temple might stand on a purified piece of land. Afterwards, as we have already seen, a temple was built to be later buried, and over top of these ruins a new temple was raised to the cult.

There is a hypothesis that the oval floor plan was reserved for temples dedicated to female divinities. These would then recall the first holy sites in history, which were always partially buried and were traditionally interpreted as dwelling places of the mother goddesses.

It could be possible that the oval temples were meant to evoke the Primal Waters, whose outer limits suggest the shape of a large womb. Perhaps they were to point to an original space as well, conceived as a territory from which all others would arise. In this way cities would exist thanks to the generative presence of these maternal temples.

In two of the three cases, however, we seem to find the logic that would connect a type of holy place with a type of deity: primal feminine deities like Inanna, goddess of creation and destruction, and Ninhursag, goddess of the mountains. Both temples, surrounded as they were by a wall whose curve could have suggested a female shape, might have looked like the powerfully mysterious bodies of clay statues depicting goddesses, priestesses and "queens", though this explanation could be somewhat simplistic.

Perhaps we will never be able to understand what these temples were really about, as their archeological remains have worn down to the ground with the passing of time.

Temples in Mesopotamia and Greece

In almost all cultures temples are a world unto themselves. They make up part of visible reality, yet represent either the empyreal sphere (where the deities dwell) or the cosmos. Upon occasion, their floor plans reflect the movement of some sidereal being held to be the visible manifestation of a given god.

The layout of ancient temples has led to speculations of a frequently esoteric or gratuitous nature. It was quite common to build temples in line with the arrangement of celestial bodies. Planets, stars and particularly bright constellations were used as reference points. Venus (which was mistakenly taken to be a morning or evening star), the North Star or Ursa Major, or just as well the Pleiades star cluster near Orion's Belt, were the most commonly used references from the night sky in arranging holy spaces. Perhaps this was because they were easy to find, or was due to their position being relatively unchanging.

The cardinal directions have also been used as referential orientation points. The main façade of a Greek temple always looked east, so that the rising sun could illuminate the face of the cult's statue when the temple doors were opened. This was how the god in question came into contact with himself. In contrast, the façades of Gothic churches look to the west, so that the morning sun coming in through the stained glass windows of the apse might light the faces of the faithful as they move down the aisle towards the altar. The Christian church is the dwelling place of man, while the pagan temple is the place of the divinity.

The Mesopotamian temple also respected the cardinal directions. An essential difference, however, is that the corners of the building face them rather than the façades. While the Greek temple is subordinated to these points and so inserts itself into the cosmos, becoming its replica, the Mesopotamian temple signals to them, marking their position. The corners thus work as arrowheads aiming at the cardinal directions, making them visible. The temple is not then molded into the cosmos nor does it work as its image; it is, instead, what founds the cosmos.

The Mesopotamian cosmos is rectangular or square, with four corners. The heavenly vault has a square floor plan and is set upon four columns.

Space, therefore, needs four points to arrange itself, and it is the temple that marks them out.

The Sumerian temple is comparable to a net laid over the land. It is like a perfectly woven cloth keeping space safe, not letting it return to a state of primal chaos. Without the temple, the organized world would not exist; it is the mechanism that defines it, arranges it and makes it last. The relationship between the cosmos and the temple is, in this way, turned upside down: first comes the temple, and only then can the cosmos be conceived and consequently come into being.

The Tower of Babel and the Mesopotamian Ziggurat

All works of art reinterpret a previous creation, offering a different point of view or dealing with aspects that were left unresolved, which then might act as motifs. This work of art's new meaning should then alter that of the previous one, exposing its latent features. In this way each new creation unveils unseen aspects of artworks from before. In such a sequence of events, where every artwork is taken as the revision of a previous one and the fount for what is to follow, we are led to a variety of meanings, all of them valid, while exposing the complex relationships between what is visible and invisible.

The Tower of Babel is one of the earliest reinterpretations of a previous creation. As described in the Book of Genesis, it is a structure inspired by the ziggurat of the main temple in the city of Babylon, dedicated to the god Marduk, the city's guardian. The buildings were formally similar, even though Babel solely existed in its Biblical account. As for the ziggurat of Babylon, only traces of its foundations have been found. Both structures have taken on an imaginary status in the present.

The ziggurat of the Temple of Marduk, erected in the seventh century BC, was a stepped pyramid making up part of a sacred enclosure. It was placed beside the temple itself, and was surrounded by courtyards, ponds and trees. It was in turn based on a prototype, the ziggurat of the temple of the moon god in the city of Ur, conceived and built around the year 2100 BC.

We do not know for sure what the ziggurat's function was. It is clear, however, that it was not a tomb like the Egyptian pyramids, nor an astronomical observatory, which is what we find with the Mayan pyramids. One possibility was that it worked as the elevated base of the main chapel where the statue for cult worship was erected.

If this were the case, the ziggurat was designed as a support to keep the god's dwelling place as far from the human world as possible. While the divinity had descended to the land of the living, he nonetheless could not touch the ground, as that would turn him into a mortal and strip him of his divine status. This is why it was so important for the god to be received in a celestial dwelling, where no human being (except kings and certain priests) had ventured. In this way the ziggurat symbolized the substantial difference between mortals and immortals. It was the expression of human inferiority and submission, as people bowed before divine grandeur, prostrated before a god whose dwelling place was on high.

The Tower of Babel, in contrast, was given a quite different set of meanings. Though built by humans like the ziggurat, it resembled a mountain whose task was to link heaven and earth. While the ziggurat was a descending stairway, used solely by the god to approach when attending the petitions of men, the Tower of Babel was a stairway to be climbed—and here those ascending it were men striving to match the gods (to reach Yahweh), and so raise themselves to their level. In this way the Tower of Babel was a sign of pride and not submission, proving human beings did not have a particularly strong notion of there being some great abyss between heaven and earth.

The fate of both towers was nonetheless the same: both fell, in one case brought down by time, in the other taken down by the god in question, enraged by the arrogance of man.

In Mesopotamia cataclysms, wars and all evils, along with the very decadence of cities, were caused by the gods, who would suddenly turn their backs on men and abandon them as punishment for some error. A serious mistake by a king would be chastised with the gods retiring their protection from the city, which would summarily be sacked by its enemies. When a city was laid siege to and fell, and when all its buildings were burnt and destroyed, the message was clear: divine destiny had turned against the inhabitants.

The question remains, then, as to whether the decline of the Babylonian ziggurat and the fall of the Tower of Babel were brought on by different causes. The ziggurat was not erected by men who thought they were gods, though ended up being razed for the impiety of a king who believed himself a god. Humans throughout Mesopotamian history always saw themselves as soft clay figurines, easily dissolved at the slightest slip. Placing oneself at the level of the gods was an unforgiveable offense, to be punished by death and the destruction of the city. This would also bring with it the logical destruction of the ziggurat, having become a useless structure blurring the previously sharp line between gods and mortals.

What would a ziggurat be good for if the great divide between gods and men were not upheld?

It is possible that the difference between the ziggurat and the Tower of Babel was not that great after all. In both cases the construction itself served to question the idea of a perfect hierarchical structure meant to mediate between gods and humans. Such hierarchies have always been put in doubt in the process of building, as architecture has always been a show of human pride. Depending upon the value placed on such a sin or virtue, what you thought of what architecture expressed or deserved would change. Art has always been a way for men to believe themselves gods, and still is. Maybe this is something that is simply inevitable.

The Threshold

The most important parts of a Mesopotamian building were the foundation and the threshold. Both features were set below ground, with the foundation not even visible. As stone was scarce in the region of the Tigris and Euphrates Delta, the walls and even the foundation were done with sun-dried bricks. The structures were thus occasionally vulnerable to unforeseeable flooding that could regularly plague the region. Any architectural features meant to last, to defend the building from falling into the hands of its attackers (or to evil spirits), had to be cut in stone. Yet this would not be enough. It was also important to inscribe formulas into the stone guaranteeing the building had indeed been erected by the king under the auspices of the protecting gods.

The threshold was one of the few parts of any building of prestige to be built in stone. It was a delicate part of any construction project. Still today, it is the place where ritual actions related to the flow from public to private space are held. There is a different set of rules for the threshold: take off your shoes, remove your hat, take off your coat, and so on. It is a space that marks out limits, though it also puts the inside and the outside in touch, connecting the domestic sphere to urban space. In Sumer, prayers and curses written in stone were done with the idea of driving evil away.

The threshold was so important that if for any reason the king chose to physically move a building to another place, he would ensure that the foundation stones and those comprising the threshold of the then-unused structure were taken to the new site, regardless of their weight. In a certain sense, these components of a previous building would become the "essence" of the building meant to be rebuilt. For the new structure to endure and relate appropriately with its surroundings, as if it had not been physically moved at all, the previous foundation and threshold stones would be used again in the new building. Until that time they had fulfilled their role perfectly well by protecting the life of the previous palace or temple.

A single stone could make a building come alive; a simple threshold set into the floor was enough to set the space apart, distinguishing the inside from the outside. The strip of border symbolized by the threshold, to be crossed over with care, had to be preserved forever, so as to ensure that chaos would not return to the earth and mix the domestic with the public sphere, for that was precisely what had happened in the early times when the world had yet to be inhabited.

The Brick of Destiny

It seemed to be a customary practice in Sumerian construction, to use a *sig₄-nam-ta-ra*. This rather enigmatic object has given rise to a variety of interpretations.

The translation of the term varies depending upon who is doing it: *sig₄* was a brick, though also a limit or a boundary, a foundation or a base. *Tar*, as an adjective, meant "judicious", while as verb it was "to establish" or "to search". As for the verbal expression *nam tar*, it is usually translated as "to establish the destiny of". *Sig₄-nam-ta-ra* would thus be "the brick of destiny".

Present-day knowledge of Sumerian grammar and vocabulary does not allow us to know for sure what this object might have been. Was it something that expressed a destiny? An object meant for a specific function?

Translators tend to opt for the former version, making it the "brick of destiny". The use of this object was given special emphasis by the Neo-Sumerian king Gudea during the reconstruction of Ningirsu's temple. The Sumerians placed great importance on the "first brick", equivalent to our "cornerstone". It was a very large brick, which unlike conventional rectangular ones could be square, and it measured up to 20 x 20 x 2 inches. During its manufacture a pre-established ritual was followed using special instruments, and the adobe base was mixed with materials held to have magical or symbolic value, like milk, butter, olive oil, honey and beer, amongst others. The manufacture, transportation and placement of the brick was the responsibility of the king.

This "foundational" brick would have what was often a rather long inscription on it. The phrase could include a description of the foundational ritual itself, making mention of the monarch's grandeur and piety. It could feature a prayer to the gods, calling on them to protect the holy site. There could also be a curse written on it against anyone who might dare destroy the temple. A few copies would be made of the brick, and it would usually be placed in the building's foundation and along different sections of the walls.

The brick of destiny could thus be a foundational brick. Even so, some researchers argue that the object had a different function, that it was used either to signal the building's placement or to state what the construction project's function was. In this latter case we could be talking about an administrative or religious document, something like a property title—only divine.

Not all experts agree that we are in fact speaking about a brick for construction at all. It could have been a tablet, molded and produced in series, used for an inscription that might well have been the project's architectural plan. The tablets would have then been a foundational tool for construction, since such documents were set into the base of the building before it was erected. The building would then be built over its plan, in a way resembling what is done nowadays with the placement of an honorary cornerstone, which often contains the drafted plans for the building. Both these visual documents and the tablets of destiny held the future building within them, containing everything needed for its subsequent construction.

Some researchers argue that the brick of destiny was a way of metonymically designating the building, given that it both announced it and contained a scale version of it. A brick of destiny would in that way be a plan, whose function was to proclaim the good news that a building would be constructed on that site.

The Sumerians prefigured an architectural current that has been common ever since the sixteenth century, where construction itself is not considered necessary. A brick of destiny is an ideal building, and would always be the true one. It is the salvation of architecture and of all humans found therein.

Mesopotamian Space

The most common Sumerian term for "space" is $muš_3$, while in Akkadian it is $mātu$. Even so, these translations do not reflect what the Mesopotamians understood by space, as their concept was closer to the Greek idea than to the seventeenth century European view. Indeed, $muš_3$ had two other spatial meanings: "flat earth" and "holy place". The flatland was Mesopotamia, or, more precisely, the land stretching from Babylon to the Persian Gulf between the Tigris and Euphrates rivers. Mesopotamian territory was set between the foothills of the Zagros Mountains to the east and the desert to the west of the Euphrates River, from the start of the Taurus Mountains to the north all the way down to the Persian Gulf. The area was indeed so flat that the rivers struggled to make their way to the sea, winding and turning as their courses shifted or flooded over with subtle changes in the terrain.

The Mesopotamian notion of space brings together all known and inhabited space. It was the space populated by Mesopotamian tribes, a least until the first millennium BC.

The fact that this space corresponded to the land they were from is seen in the Akkadian word $mātu$, which literally means just that: "native land". This term is also translated as "inhabitants", since the space could not be conceived without human life. It is a space where humans choose to live.

However much this concept seems to anticipate the Platonic idea of space, it should be qualified, since the most customary translation of $muš_3$ is "holy place". It refers to the enclosed part of a religious structure, an area set off from the rest that could well include a temple. We are not speaking of abstract space but of consecrated space. This space belongs to the gods and can only be conceived as including some sort of supernatural presence.

It turns out that $muš_3$ has a third meaning, which might seem unsettling at first: it is translated as "face" or "appearance". Yet it never refers to a human face, always having to do with a divine one. $Muš_3$ is the visible manifestation of a god, which in principle would be necessarily invisible.

The gods only needed to materialize themselves when dealing with human beings. Such an "incarnation" could only take place in a holy place, and was expressed by means of the sudden appearance of a face. The divine face, and especially its eyes, irradiated light. In this way space spread out as far as the splendorous divine glow could reach, setting out the limits of the temple, coinciding with the incarnate god's field of vision.

Conceived in this way, space would no longer be the "native land", but would refer instead to an area exclusively given over to the god. If we recall that the temples were divine dwelling places, humans were quite logically not authorized to enter into them.

Besides this, the gods did not manifest themselves arbitrarily. They would make themselves visible for humans such as kings and priests, who would in turn announce the news of the deity's arrival to his temple to the city. In this way, space was conceived as a site where humans could hold out the hope that one day the gods would illuminate them while simultaneously revealing themselves.

Space is not an abstract concept; rather, it is linked to the hopes and desires of humans. It refers to a site where humans might wait for a better life, an authentic life, necessarily rooted in the native land.

AESTHETICS

The Image and the Model

One of the epithets of Enki, the Mesopotamian god of architecture, was *mummu*, meaning "mold"; it referred to creative capacity. The word is related to the Akkadian *ummu*, meaning "mother", and *ummatum*, which means "son".

In Mesopotamia molds were used for baking bread, and in manufacturing the majority of artistic items, including small statuettes, fetish objects, clay amulets and fine ceramics. Even the most repeated texts, such as the hymns, prayers and curses written on foundational bricks, were printed with molded roller stamps.

The now-familiar difference between an original and a replica did not exist. The idea was that figurines made from a mold had not been created but rather engendered. The basin the cast objects were taken from was related to Nammu, the primal goddess and mother of Enki, though the word *nammu* also meant "vagina".

All creative processes unite nature and manual work. In Akkadian mythology, Enki, molder of the world, made fourteen statuettes with clay taken from the womb of the goddess Nammu. He then placed them into fourteen holy vaginas so that they would be transformed after nine months gestation into the first seven pairs of human beings.

The idea was that the resemblance between the fabricated piece and the original mold corresponded to the similarity between a child and its parents, so that the parent-child relationship was set up as the model for all artistic creation. The work of art was produced using the same generative process as found in real life. That is why images were intimately connected to the reality they represented, even when incarnating invisible powers. This explains the fetishistic, magical value the ancients put on images, whether on statues or in paintings.

There is no difference between an original and a copy done from a mold. In Akkadian, the word meaning "image", *tamšiltu*, also means "likeness", with this term closely related to the term referring to a mold, *tamšiltu*.

The high value placed on these small statues contributed to the magical conception of the mimetic image. The statuettes were doubles taken from their models; they were granted the same powers and were thought to be deserving of identical treatment. It was a sacrilege to mistreat them, a veritable crime, since the damage done to the statue was passed on to the original model.

This symbiosis between the image and the model as founded on a family relationship was also predominant in Greece, and was especially common in the early Christian period, where Jesus Christ was the son of God the Father, made in his image. In Greek, *typos* meant both "son" and "image", and especially referred to an image resembling its model, as what happens when producing from a mold. The *typos* and the prototype were taken to be identical. This was why Father and Son, though different persons, were the same being. This same relationship was reiterated in more or less the same way between the Son and his iconic image, between the Man and his painted portrait, which would therefore have to be venerated.

The Image and its Double

Plato reflected on what he called the paradox of mimesis. In order for the mimetic image to be accepted, it should look as much as possible like the model it was meant to mirror. The problem lay in how far the limit of physical and psychological resemblance could be pushed. Once the image came to coincide point by point with its referential model, as if a mirror image, and if it were then given life itself (like what occurred with the female statue made by Pygmalion, transfigured into a human being by the goddess Venus), in what way would it differ from the model? The answer is that it would not differ at all. As a consequence, the ontological difference between image and model would vanish, and the creation of the duplicate would emerge as a problem of public order. The earth's population could end up doubling and confusion would reign. Nobody would know with what or who they were dealing, be it an original referential model or its duplicate.

The principal god of Babylon, Marduk, son of Enki the god of architecture, would thus proclaim: "I was able to finish the ziggurat of the great temple of Babylon, a copy [*gaba-ri*] of the Primal Waters."

Gabarû, in Akkadian, is translated as "image" or "replica". This term comes from the Sumerian *gaba-ri*, which was understood as a secondary relationship with the image, translated at times as "copy of a document". Nevertheless, the first meaning of *gaba-ri* was not related to art but to war, and is translated as "rival" or "opponent". In effect, *gaba* means "up against", or refers to a rival's courage. In itself, *ri* means "to deploy" or "to project". Therefore, *gaba-ri* referred to an equal who one opposed. A battle is where warriors come face to face with each other, seeing an image of themselves in their opponent. They know they are not different in any way, and that is their reason for fighting.

In contrast, the god Ningirsu proclaimed the following:

> En gaba-ri nu-tuku
> Gudea Cylinder A, IX, 22

"I do not have [*nu-tuku*] a lord [*en*] of the same [*gaba-ri*]", that is, I have no rival, no one is as good as me; I am unique. Combat can only take place between equals, for a confrontation between unequal warriors dishonors the winner if he is truly superior, while if the winner were the inferior rival it would constitute a sacrilege. Only hierarchically and (perhaps) morally similar beings can look each other in the eye and take each other on in battle, like two inexplicably estranged brothers.

In this way a real *gaba-ri*, a vivid image of the monarch, was a threat to the kingdom, precisely because he had all the physical and moral qualities to put the king in check and supplant him. A *gaba-ri* fought to the death with the defender of public order. It is true that a *gaba-ri* was a flesh and blood double, in no way different from the person he had before him. He could be considered a perfect reflection of the king, who he confronted on the battlefield and sought to replace.

Plato set out the problems a mimetic image could cause in the world, although the idea had already been seen in its nascent state in Mesopotamia, where it was understood that no two entities could be equal without warranting a rivalry. As soon as they appeared before each other, confrontation was inevitable, as danger reared its head and threatened to overturn established order. The presence of an equal added a perilous imbalance to the equation.

At the same time, rivals and images were needed to ensure the coherence of the world. Without a worthy rival, one's true worth could never be measured, as King Gilgamesh learnt with the appearance of Enkidu, his "soulmate". A mimetic image is a necessary reflection, giving us back the image of what we are (however much we may refuse to see it).

Ever since Plato placed the *eideai* in the empyrean, the relationship between the divine and the idea has given rise to complex, never-ending theological arguments. *Eideai* in Greek meant "form", whether ideal or disembodied, form willing to materialize itself in its descent to earth.

In Mesopotamia heaven too was inhabited by ideal, divine beings, though without as many conflicts and ambiguities as in Greece. In spite of this (or perhaps because of it), the ontological structure of Mesopotamia was closer to our own than we might have imagined.

The Idea and the Gods

Šag₄ was a common Sumerian word referring to a vital organ: the heart. *šag₄* (or *šà*) also makes up part of various spatial expressions, like *šà...ak-šè*, translated as "inside of", and *šà...ak-ta*, meaning "in the midst of". It refers to a real or conceptual entity hidden within a greater one. This is why, if we consider a work of art to be the sum of a visible shape and the content expressed through it, *šag₄* would be the meaning concealed within a created shape; it is translatable as "idea". Thus *šag₄* is the closest term we have to the Platonic concept of the idea, if such a similitude can be made.

Many Sumerian works were produced from prototypes. The preexistence of a non-material entity demonstrated they had mental images their creations were made from.

In Sumer the kings ruled, but the gods did as well. Things were done because the gods so willed. In this way *šag₄* was divine will and desire, the god's creative volition. It was something like an ideal form from which all things were materialized.

Šag₄ ("will", "desire", "mental image", "heart") intervened in all of creation, which took place in two phases, one in heaven and the other on earth. The first had it projected out beyond the god, giving way to a heavenly model, a prototype, but not a miniature. It was an ideal model in perfect correlation to its material expression, even when it came to size.

The history of the creation of the temple of Ningirsu reflects this process faithfully. The protecting guardian of Lagash comes to King Gudea in his dreams, commanding the monarch to build a temple in his honor, following the visual and written instructions received. In his autobiography, the Neo-Sumerian Gudea explains how difficult it had been for him to decipher the plans for the temple's construction. The commands (and with them the visual and written documents) were not clear enough to be properly interpreted, and Gudea required the assistance of various gods, including his mother Nanshe, goddess of writing and of heavenly planimetrics. Gudea was aware that the phrase sent to him by the god had a profound double meaning, which could not be captured on first impression.

It had to be interpreted in such a way as to get to its core, to the final, true meaning, with the help of the goddess of exegetes. This is why Gudea would plead:

Šag$_4$-bi ha-ma-pad$_3$-de$_3$
Gudea Cylinder A, III, 28

This short phrase is absolutely pivotal. The term *šag$_4$* appears in it, though in this case it does not mean "heart"; rather, it refers to something inside that enlivens. The phrase thus means: "Let the meaning of the dream be revealed to me."

Šag$_4$ in this context takes on a new sense, referring to the content of a message. This information is conceived as something hidden that should be revealed. The goddess Nanshe is especially gifted in this "hermeneutic" task, as she is the deity who reads messages in the stars. Along with this, the message content is like a vital organ, the heart of the text, expressing a crucial meaning that influences its receiver.

The orders transmitted were so precise that an ideal model was formed even before the material construction had begun. This model was "founded" by *an-na*, a term that could just as well be translated as "An, father of the gods", or "in heaven". So we do not know for sure if this model was the creation of the father-god or a heavenly doing, although most likely both meanings were valid, as the father god An was concomitant with heaven and fully inhabited it.

Of course this "ideal" creation came from *šag$_4$*, from divine will. If the divinity in question had been An, if the will to create had been his, the internal idea and the external model would have fully coincided, since An comprised the entire heavenly vault. His ideas, then, and his models, were necessarily contained in him. In a certain sense, the Supreme Being An had no need for the ideal model to be mediated. His will and his idea were expressed directly on earth, they came down from heaven and incarnated themselves in matter. His will was a command that would inevitably be fulfilled.

For all this, $\check{s}\grave{a}g_4$ was not only a divine entity, as it belonged to humans as well (Gudea Cylinder A, I, 27). Or at least they had the gift of being able to find it in objects: it was the content of things. For this reason $\check{s}ag_4$—the idea—was both in humans and in things created by them, and this was clearly a reflection of the divine $\check{s}ag_4$. What man sought in "works of art" was a divine idea, wrapped up inside the work by the god and revealed by virtue of man's good judgment.

$\check{S}ag_4$ was thus variegated: it was there amongst the gods and in heaven; it was a preexistent celestial entity; and it was also found in men and in things created on earth, in consonance with an ideal model.

This is why it is possible to state that the full complexity of the creative act, whose analysis runs through the theory of art from Greece up to the present, was already enunciated in Sumer, where the architect's action was its prototype. Just as in our day, in Sumer the relationship between what is made and what is dreamt, between impulses (divine inspiration) and limitations, was fully accounted for.

The Divine Image

Unlike what happens with Egyptian, Greek and Roman mythology, there are few visual images of gods to complement Mesopotamian mythology. This could be attributable to some random factor related to the archeological digs, though still today we do not know what the gods looked like, leaving us to imagine them on the basis of written documents. In this way, Mesopotamian culture is able to step around visual culture's radical inability (in painting, sculpture, photography and cinema) to make it possible for what is visible and invisible to share the same space.

Every time an artist has tried to bring two substantially different realities into the same picture plane, both of them have lost their specificity. What is celestial becomes overly carnal and obvious, while what is visible takes on an illusory air, making it seem even more distant. This problem is not as grave in Christianity, since the heavenly powers were incarnated, and so became fully human. We are not sure if such powers still remained divine. In Greco-Roman depictions of them, the indolent gazes of the gods made them seem absent, closer to inhuman than superhuman.

It could be said that the painters and sculptors of the Pharaohs were aware of the problem and tried to neutralize any excess sense of proximity in anthropomorphic figuration by having them take on animal traits. The Egyptians brought the gods back to their own world, even while accepting that their figuration was not naturalistic. It was clear to them that the gods did not really have the aberrant appearance seen in their depictions; by no means were they like monsters. Representations of them were symbolic, as the heavenly powers could not be portrayed. All you could do was evoke them by means of shocking imagery alluding to their many superhuman powers. They were precisely what human beings are not and do not want to be.

Very few visual images of Mesopotamian deities have come down to us, which does not necessarily mean that the art of Mesopotamia was aniconic. Many texts refer to religious statues made with precious metals, though they were likely melted down for other uses thousands of years ago. It is possible that naturalist imagery was used exclusively for visible shapes and beings, kings included, who notwithstanding their heroic grandeur were rarely taken to be divine. The gods, at least in the beginning, were habitually invoked by means of emblems, or through empty alcoves at the back of chapels, alluding to their veiled presence. On the other hand, certain reliefs found on cylinder seals (roller stamps) have been interpreted as representing divine beings, even though there is no textual corroboration for this thesis. The majority of statuettes assumed to be representing gods, like on iron or bronze foundation pegs or small, clay amulets, were evidence of "popular" art pertaining to the world of magic.

Such pieces were not made to be seen but to be buried under the foundation or within the walls of a building. Most of the ancient statues found do not depict gods but rather humans making offerings, and some experts believe they were not cast before the second millennium. It would seem that the large statues supposedly representing supernatural beings were from the outer limits of Sumer, from areas on the outskirts of the delta and chronologically late in time.

This is why the only thing left to Mesopotamian gods (or perhaps the only thing they ever had) were the images their names evoked and still do. Like with these images, in profane portraiture what established the relationship with the model was the inscribed name and not the resemblance. Only the name made it possible for the image to replace the person.

The graven image does not have the word's ability to evoke what is invisible and carry it over to a tangible plane. In spite of its search for transcendence, even abstract art of the twentieth century, while avoiding the representation of earthly shapes and beings, was little more than a placid and pleasant (or confused and disturbing) play of decorative forms. It was mostly incapable of "expressing" transcendence—as excessively large canvases do not necessarily awaken sublime or mystic sensations—making it a faulty adventure, demonstrating the inability of visual or sculpted images, naturalistic or abstract, to go beyond what is evident. The word, in contrast, as seen in twentieth century novels, is more than capable of gathering and transcribing the most hermetic shifts and aspirations of the soul. The Sumerian word comes down to us from a remote period in time, wrapped in the mystery of never being fully deciphered, charged with the most appropriate ineffability when referring to the beyond.

Art and Beauty

Dù, ĝar and *dim* are the three most common Sumerian verbs, customarily rendered as "to make" or "to build". *Ĝar* is used above all to designate preparatory work, such as in the placement of a building's foundation. *Dù* means "to mold", as well as "to construct". *Dim* means "to manufacture", although it is translated as the generic verb for "to construct" or "to build" (usually *sidim* is taken to be "architect" or "builder"), which *dù* also encompasses.

Regardless, *dim* brings with it an interesting twist: it also meant "to decorate". Embellishment was obtained by means of work, by "art". Ornamentation's goal was to better express aesthetic qualities. An example of this is the work done on the façades of temples. The thick adobe brick walls were laced with small cones of glazed stone paste, with a full range of golden tones shining back at the harsh Mesopotamian sunlight.

There does not seem to be a Sumerian equivalent for the modern idea of beauty. What is usually translated as "handsome" or "beautiful" is the term *galam-kad$_5$*, which literally refers to artistic work. We could also translate it as "well-made". Perhaps what *galam-kad$_5$* suggested for the Sumerians could be understood if we consider that *kad$_5$* meant "to tie", "to bound" or "to interlock". An object described as *galam-kad$_5$* was "well-finished", where each and every one of its features was in place. The model of any work considered *galam-kad$_5$* would have likely been a piece of cloth, with the warp and woof tightly woven together. In this way, in Sumerian reality and in its imagination, the "first" architectural constructions were made with braided reeds where the interwoven walls resembled carpeting. *Galam-kad$_5$* was especially used to describe well-made architectural structures, referring above all to their floor plans. In a certain sense, *galam-kad$_5$* was said of an object that had clearly been well-ordered, something worked on in detail, something carefully manufactured. It referred to a work where independent features carefully applied resulted in beautifully balanced surface motifs.

The Akkadian translation of the Sumerian verb *dim* reaffirms this idea: *banû* is translated as "to create", "to construct" or "to erect". Artistic creation for the Akkadians had specifically architectural composition as its point of reference (it was the same for the Sumerians).

Creation meant building a city. Yet *banû* had other meanings as well. It is also translated as "to work well", or just as commonly, "to work for good". This association between art and morality was corroborated by the third meaning given to *banû*, though here we are dealing with an adjective: "beautiful", as well as "good".

Ethics and aesthetics were unified fields, and would continue to be so for thousands of years. Both in Greece and later Rome *agathos* ("good-looking", "noble") and *bonus* (meaning "good", "high quality") were used both for the appearance of something and for the aims of an action.

Something comparable to our idea of beauty, if such a similitude were possible, was not found naturally in Mesopotamia; what was beautiful was the fruit of one's labor. Nature was good and replete, vital and abundant; it pleased the senses, though it was not properly speaking "beautiful".

The Western concept of beauty is quite different. Nature, as a work of God, must always be more beautiful than any human creation, which in turn would always be somehow tainted. Even the builders of cathedrals were deemed to have made some sort of deal with the devil, who as the name suggests (*diabole* in Greek meant "division") dreamt of smashing God's work into thousands of little pieces.

The Sumerian *dim*, the Akkadian *banû* and the Greek *technao* were used for describing divine creation and human as well. The Hebrew religion is unique in giving divine action and human action each a different name. In the Bible Yahweh created and engendered, *bara'*, while men were left to build, *banah*. The Bible abounds with contrary opinions and warnings against human making. Painting is held to resemble what prostitutes do when putting makeup on. Statues led to idolatry and had to be torn down. Even though Jesus was the son of a carpenter, opinions like these held strong throughout most of Puritan Christianity, which was also influenced by classicism's disparagement of the craftsman and the Platonic censure of mimesis.

In the West, it would take until the eighteenth century for "artistic" or "manufactured" beauty to regain the status it had enjoyed in Mesopotamia.

Even so, the Enlightenment was the period when art lost its ability to reveal the mysteries of man and of the world, turning into an expendable decorative task whose cognitive function was taken over by science. The supposed rise of artistic beauty never really happened. Works of art were beautiful indeed, though they were good for nothing. This was why we would be able to live without art—and without beauty as well. Kant himself had the suspicion that artistic beauty was banal, given its highest expression was seen in finely groomed gardens. Horticulture was art's summum—and the pastime of the leisure class, as Voltaire knew only so well.

Judeo-Christian wariness of beauty's uselessness or malignity continues to persist, as contemporary artists strive to remind us daily. The destiny of the West would have been quite different if the Mesopotamian vision of human making had held sway.

Aesthetics

Aesthetics, or art theory, implies the existence of a type of object that has been conceived and created both for sensual pleasure and to stimulate thought amongst those contemplating it. These objects are in principle set apart from those that meet a need. The first such objects were defined from the eighteenth century onwards as works of art, while the second were considered to be craft or functional objects. This clear difference between art and craft is no more than three centuries old.

Almost five thousand years old, Mesopotamian (and above all Sumerian) art should be situated within the framework of what we call useful art. Nothing was produced for mere sensory pleasure, as everything fulfilled a function: to assist, to sustain, to protect, to cover or to gather, amongst a wide range of possibilities. This does not mean that objects did not arouse emotions, and by no means does it signify that sensory aims were secondary.

To speak of aesthetics in relation to Sumerian culture, when they had no concept of "art for art's sake", perhaps does not make too much sense. There are, of course, no treatises on art from the time: there is no such thing as Mesopotamian art theory. Furthermore, it seems that there was no term that could be clearly translated as "beauty". This does not mean that the Mesopotamians were not "sensitive" to form, color or the "content" of certain works. By studying their production we are able to detect evaluative criteria as related to their tastes.

It would seem on the one hand that they prized technical skill (particularly excellent execution endured as a valid standard in other cultures until the twentieth century). The quality of a "well-made" object was equally derived from the effort put into it, the practice in doing so, and from divine "grace". It was held that the gods either directly or indirectly inspired certain producers, even to the point of actively intervening in their production. In such latter cases, divine splendor was duly transferred to the object being worked on.

This idea fits with another of the qualities most appreciated by the Sumerians: the "shiny veneer" of the work, a material quality that was above all related to spiritual values. Certain works were able to truly shine. Color and sheen, when accomplished with skill, evoked the divine presence, which had inspired the human maker to work with effort and control. It could be said that the Mesopotamians, like much later the Christians and Muslims (all of them emerging out of the East) preferred the aesthetics of light over the aesthetics of proportion, while this latter was predominant in Greece. Yet above all they appreciated the spiritual "sheen" of a work, the glow the gods would endow particularly "fortunate" pieces with; this was not always expressed in a material way, though it would always be something ineffable. We are speaking of a quality resembling a divine aura, something still seen with certain Christian icons.

Sumerian works of art had specific aims. The temples were the dwelling places of the gods, while jewelry would accompany the deceased person in transit to the beyond. Yet they also met less defined ends, as "art" sought to make life more joyful and assist in the relationship between humans and gods. In a certain sense, art brought them closer together, or at least would assuage the sense humans had of heaven's indifference towards humanity. The work of art was a form of consolation. The pleasure derived from it replaced the joy heaven should rightly have provided though rarely in fact did. In this way, works crafted with divine grace gave rise to admiration while arousing fear or awe, expressing emotions similar to what Hellenistic art, or the Roman Christian later on, would seek. What we are saying is that they expressed feelings that were not that different from the sense of the sublime, where pleasure, joy, uncertainty and fear were all brought together.

The Foundational Poem of Gilgamesh

The great Sumerologist Piotr Michalowski came up with a new interpretation of the *Epic of Gilgamesh* and its contribution to fiction and culture. The epic poem tells the story of the king's discovery of mortality and the further revelation that death need not necessarily lead to being forgotten.

After surviving the flood Utnapishtim tells Gilgamesh about a plant with the power of everlasting life, though the king loses the plant and fails in his attempt to revive his faithful friend Enkidu from the dead. The ghost of Enkidu appears before Gilgamesh and tells him of his dire existence in the underworld, revealing how human mortality makes him different from the immortal gods. After a long voyage that takes him to the ends of the earth, the king returns home. Once in front of the city wall, he realizes that he had built the city of Uruk, that it was his doing. In this way he is reassured he will not fall into oblivion, since the city he had raised would endure, keeping the memory of its founder alive.

The *Epic of Gilgamesh* concludes with the king's words of admiration for his own accomplishments. Michalowski goes further than this in his interpretation of the text, as the poem closes with a set of verses whose meaning has never been fully appreciated. Gilgamesh speaks to Urshanabi, the night watchman:

> Go up, Urshanabi, onto the wall of Uruk and walk around.
> Examine its foundation...
> *Epic of Gilgamesh, 11:15*

The Mesopotamian kings would customarily preside over the foundational rites of buildings and cities. Printed tablets have been found amongst the votive objects placed in the trenches dug for the foundations of constructed walls. The texts appearing on them narrate the habitual foundational rite, extolling the king who had ordered the respective city to be built.

Given that the foundational rite of Uruk did not vary from what was traditionally the case, tablets were placed in the foundations of the city's outer walls, with texts narrating the life, work and miracles of Gilgamesh. That is, the entire *Epic of Gilgamesh* had been buried there, with its discovery converting the king into a character of literary fame. This is in fact how Gilgamesh reached immortality, and not because his constructed projects would survive him; what has endured is the story of his life. By having his life become a fictional tale, Gilgamesh would achieve legendary status, which will last for however long his story is told.

The foundational texts written on tablets buried in building foundations were recovered when the structures had to be rebuilt. The story was then ritually recited as part of the revival ceremony, so that the building might be as splendorous as it had been in the beginning. The foundational text of Uruk tells of the creation of the text itself, with this latter telling an interminable tale where creation narrates itself. We are speaking of a circular narrative that concludes with the written fixation of the text itself, containing the poem of its very writing.

In this way King Gilgamesh, observing and narrating his own experiences from a distance, turns himself into an immortal character. The work that truly immortalized him was his own life, turned into a literary subject while he was still alive. Or better said: his mortality was overcome by the possibility of continually reading his autobiography forever more.

Gilgamesh lived to become a literary character of his own creation, prefiguring the playful ruse we find in the second volume of *Don Quixote*, where the ingenious *hidalgo* lives to tell his own life, thus turning himself into a fictional character, standing in his own place.

Perhaps, as Michalowski would explain, there is no more subtle literary creation than this poem. It is a text whose structure makes it an unforeseeable precedent to Proust's *In Search of Lost Time*. It is indeed unfortunate that the poem is no longer taught in schools, as if it were somehow outdated, when in fact Gilgamesh endures as a faithful mirror in which to look upon our very own hopes and misfortunes.

LAY OF THE LAND

Chronology

Mesopotamian culture covers a broad period of time from the fifth millennium BC to the Arab invasion in the seventh century AD. The stages of this long period do not coincide with those of Mediterranean cultures, making the unified study of Middle Eastern culture all the more difficult. Further complications arise with the study of the cultures of the Tigris and Euphrates Delta, as each small area, each city even, has its own chronology, and each is susceptible to alterations with every new archaeological discovery. It is still possible, however, to establish a general time frame.

The Neolithic, which does not end in Eastern Europe until the second millennium BC, finalizes in the Middle East in the fourth millennium BC with the founding of the city of Uruk. Over this thousand year period southern Mesopotamia is dominated by a culture that has no writing and which controls parts of the north by establishing small colonies. Its area of influence reaches as far as the Anatolian peninsula.

The third millennium BC is dominated by Sumerian, Akkadian and Neo-Sumerian cultures which arose in the center and south of Mesopotamia, from the current site of Bagdad to the Persian Gulf, and possibly reaching as far as present-day Bahrain. The Early Dynastic Period (2900-2400 BC) included the rise of Sumerian city-states, closing with the advent of the first eastern empire between 2400 and 2200 BC around the capital city of Akkad; its site has yet to be discovered. The third millennium ends with the fall of the Akkadian Empire and the independence of its city-states, which would soon fall under the controlling power of the city of Ur, giving name to what is known as the Ur III Period.

Whereas until that point in time Babylon had been a small town, from then on it would grow into a city. It became an Akkadian bastion where the language thrived as well, dominating the center and south of Mesopotamia. The second millennium is a period of alternating dominion of three great empires: Babylonia, Assyria and the Hittite Empire, with the cities of Babylon and Ashur as the focal points of power. These three empires, which were constantly at war, have a period of splendor during the first millennium around the city of Nineveh, in the Neo-Assyrian Empire, and Babylon, in the Neo-Babylonian Empire. The two cities rivaled each other in grandeur over a five-hundred-year period. The decline of these cultures came with the rise of the Persians, who from present-day Iran occupied all of the ancient Middle East, developing an Indo-European language that was quite unrelated to Sumerian or the Semitic languages. The center of power would then shift further to the east, to the city of Persepolis.

Babylon would remain a much-coveted city, which was what drove Alexander the Great to challenge the Persians and bring them to defeat. In this way Greek culture reached the East, just as previously, in the second millennium, it had made its way to the Ionian coast. The Alexandrian Empire shifted into Roman hands around the first century AD. After the fall of Rome and the decision to move the capital to Constantinople during the fourth century AD, it would become part of the Byzantine Empire. The most easterly part, from Babylon to Persepolis, would remain in the hands of the Persians' successive heirs, with the Parthians first and then the Sasanians, from the fourth century AD on.

In the seventh century AD the Arabs defeated Persia and Byzantium and put an end to some six thousand years of ancient eastern culture.

SEVENTH-FIFTH MILLENNIUM
6000-4500   Halaf Period (Anatolia: Northern and Western Mesopotamia)
6000-3700   Ubaid Period (Southern Mesopotamia)
5000   Founding of the city of Uruk

FOURTH MILLENNIUM
3700-3000   Uruk Period (including the Jemdet Nasr Period: 3100-2900)
3500   Invention of writing

THIRD MILLENNIUM
2900-2350   Early Dynastic Period
2350-2150   Akkadian Empire
2112-2004   Ur III Empire or Neo-Sumerian Period

SECOND MILLENNIUM
2000-1600   Babylonian Empire
2000-1800   Assyrian Empire
1650-1250   Mitanni Empire
1600-1200   Hittite Empire
1600-1155   Kassite Empire (capital in Babylon)
1400-1050   Middle Assyrian Empire

FIRST MILLENNIUM
900-539   Neo-Babylonian Empire
934-610   Neo-Assyrian Empire
900-550   Neo-Hittite Empire
550-330   Achaemenid Persian Empire
330- 129   Macedonian Conquest (Alexander the Great) and Seleucid
            Empire
141-224 dC Parthian Empire

MODERN ERA
476   Fall of the Western Roman Empire
395   Birth of the Byzantine Empire
224-637   Sasanian Empire
637   Beginning of the Arab invasion and end of Ancient
            Mesopotamian Culture

The Sumerian Pantheon

The name of a god could vary by city, holy site or era, although it is not always clear whether divinities with different names were the same god or not. Each city-state had its own pantheon, led by a principal divinity, and each god was related to a holy site from where it received its "personality". Some gods were recognized throughout Mesopotamia, personifying the natural powers that had been venerated since prehistory.

There were ancestral gods, new gods and mediating gods. The first of these were born from the Primal Waters, the originating matter life emerged from. Together with An, god of heaven, they were known as the Great Gods, the Anunnaki. The new gods were called Igigi. Finally, the Apkallu or demi-gods were also known as the Seven Sages.

An, the god of Heaven, was the main deity. His wife Nammu was the goddess and mother of marshes, and was also known as Ninmah and Ninhursag, Lady of the High Mountains and of the Primal Waters. An and Nammu had two sons: Enlil, the fierce god of the wind and storms; and Enki, the ingenious architect god, designer of the world. Nisaba, the goddess of the harvest and writing, was the daughter of An with Urash or Ki, goddess of the Earth.

Enki and Damkina (possibly another name of the mother goddess of the earth and the waters) gave birth to Marduk, the principal god of Babylonia. The goddess of the channels, Nanshe, was also a descendant of Enki, as was Nisaba, according to various accounts. The three siblings Marduk, Nanshe and Nisaba were heirs to Enki's skill in organizing and cultivating the land.

Enlil and his wife Ninlil engendered nocturnal gods: the Moon Nanna and Nergal, god of the underworld, continuously battered by furious storm winds. Light arose from the darkness, and four children were born to Nanna and Ningal, the Great Lady. The first was the formidable Inanna, goddess of desire and destruction, known as Ishtar in Babylonia, Aphrodite in Greece and Venus in Rome. Her sister, Ereshkigal, was the goddess of the underworld. The third child was a male, Utu, the Sun, while the last, Ninurta or Ningirsu, was a warrior god of vegetation who fought against anyone who dared endanger fields and cities.

The Apkallu were created by Enki, the god who arranged the world. They were shaped like carp, with their long beards granting them a venerable air. They lived in the Waters of Wisdom or Primal Waters of Abzu, corresponding to the southern marshlands. It was there where the temple of the god of cleverness Enki was found, in the holy city of Eridu, in the midst of the marshes. The Apkallu, spurred on by Enki, passed on their techniques for arranging and domesticating the world to humans.

Tired of cultivating the land to feed the celestial gods, the Igigi rebelled, venturing up to the heavens to replace them. The Anunnaki tried to negotiate with them and were able to shape humans as they saw fit, from then making them in charge of arduous agricultural tasks. Finally it was the Igigi who would triumph and the Anunnaki became deities of the underworld.

These latter were urban gods who had rich personalities and complex lineages. Kings and priests were dedicated to them and prayed to them for the protection of their cities. Most likely they were not the most popular of all Sumerian divinities and supernatural powers. Craftsmen, merchants, farmers and shepherds preferred the ancient gods, bound as they were to nature and to celestial phenomena, which was why they incarnated them in fetish objects and clay amulets.

Cuneiform Writing

Cuneiform writing appeared in the city of Uruk around 3500 BC, shortly before Egyptian hieroglyphic writing. It is a pictographic writing system, where drawings represent beings and customary activities. Although the Eastern peoples and the Egyptians knew of each other, there does not seem to be any link between their two forms of writing.

The habitual support material for this writing was clay tablets, as stone was scarce in the region. It was difficult to cut the signs into this material effectively, so that the flowing edges of early cuneiform were gradually simplified. Signs that were initially naturalistic were slowly transformed into abstractions using shortened horizontal, vertical and diagonal lines.

The first signs referred to objects and imitated their contours, so that the number of signs threatened to expand exponentially. Since the most common Sumerian words were single syllable, some signs began to be used only for their sound, adding to the set of existing pictograms and syllable-grams.

Sumerian is what is called an agglutinative language, where the words do not have their own function; it is not possible to distinguish between nouns, adjectives, adverbs and verbs before their contextualization. Their suffixes and prefixes in each given phrase give the words their grammatical function. The verb is the essential feature and is found at the end of the phrase, preceded by the subject and the complements. All subtleties and clarifications are brought together as single-syllable prefixes and suffixes attached to the verb. Sumerian could distinguish between animate (including the gods) and inanimate (a category which included animals), while the language had no gender.

The important part of the sentence is not the subject but the object, so that Sumerian phrases are translated literally in the passive voice. The object is the focus of attention, driving the subject's action, and the subject only exists as a function of its action's consequences.

Another characteristic of the Sumerian language is that there was no future tense. Everything that mattered was in the past, it took all the honors. Society evolved to the degree it was able to bring itself closer to this mythical, primal past. It moved forward by turning its back on the future, which was set behind it, off in the distance. What made the future danger-ous was its being unknown.

The language distinguishes between singular, plural and the singular plural, that is, a unified opinion of a crowd expressing itself as a single per-son. So as to make reading easier, some words are preceded by superscript symbols. These show what part of the speech the next word belongs to. In this way, for example, names of gods include the superscript [d], from the noun *dingir*, which means "divinity". This makes it possible to differentiate whether the word *an* refers to the celestial vault or to An, god of Heaven.

As for the numerical subscripts and accents, their only function is to help distinguish between similar-sounding words. We do not know what Sumerian sounded like, although thanks to lists of Sumerian words tran-scribed into Akkadian, we do know how they would have been pronounced by an Akkadian speaker.

Sumerian writing evolved (as might be imagined) over the fourth and third millennia. It most likely became a dead language sometime around the end of this latter period.

The main difficulty of Sumerian lies in the impossibility of decipher-ing all the words and understanding the full set of grammatical rules. Everything we know of this language is thanks to bilingual texts in Sumerian and Akkadian, a language that is close to Hebrew and Arabic, making it possible to faithfully translate it. However, no Rosetta Stone has been found for Sumerian, nor does it seem likely that this could happen, as the archaeological digs have been sacked in times of war and dismantled over decades of long-lasting excavations.

Sumerian reflects a vision of the world that is quite unlike our own. Certain undoubtedly important subtleties make little sense in our day, or are just as well fully incomprehensible. It is not possible to understand ev-erything insinuated in the texts, so that the truth-revealing subtext is quite commonly well beyond our reach.

Bibliography

Aruz, Joan (ed.). *The Art of the First Cities. The Third Millennium B.C. from the Mediterranean to the Indus*. New York: The Metropolitan Museum of Art, 2003.

Azara, Pedro (ed.). *Antes del diluvio. Mesopotamia 3500-2100 aC*. Barcelona: Polígrafa, 2012.

Azara, Pedro. *La reconstrucción del Edén. Mito y arquitectura en Oriente*. Barcelona: Gustavo Gili, 2010.

Bachelard, Gaston. *The Poetics of Space*. Boston: Beacon, 1994.

Bruschweiler, Françoise (ed.). *La ville dans le Proche Orient ancien*. Louvain: Peeters, 1983.

Castel, Corinne. "La première ville n'existe pas. La ville au Proche-Orient pré-classique, selon les archéologues (1ère partie)". In *ArchéOrient – Le Blog*. http://archeorient.hypotheses.org/4276 [Access: June 19, 2015].

Dunham Sally. "Ancient Near Eastern Architecture". In Daniel C. Snell (ed.). *A Companion to the Ancient Near East*. Malden: Blackwell, 2005, pp. 289-303.

Emberling, Geoff: "Mesopotamian Cities and Urban Process, 3500-1600 BC". In Norman Yoffee (ed.). *A World of Cities, Cambridge History of the World, vol. III: Early Cities in Comparative Perspective 4000-1200 BC*. Cambridge: Cambridge University Press, 2015, pp. 253-278.

Evans, Jean M. *The Lives of Sumerian Sculpture: An Archaeology of the Early Dynastic Temple*. Cambridge University Press, 2012.

Forest, Jean-Daniel. *Les premiers temples de la Mésopotamie (4ᵉ et 3ᵉ millé-naires)*. Oxford: BAR International Series, 765, 1999.

Frankfort, Henri. *The Art and Architecture of the Ancient Orient*. New Haven: Yale University Press, 1995.

Hallo, William W. "Antediluvian Cities". *Journal of Cuneiform Studies*, 23, 3, 1971, pp. 57-67.

Huot, Jean-Louis. *Les premiers villageois de Mésopotamie. Du village à la ville.* Paris : Armand Colin, 1994.

Huot, Jean-Louis. *Les sumériens. Entre le Tigre et l'Euphrate.* Paris: Armand Colin, 1989.

Huot, Jean-Louis; Jean-Paul Tahlmann and Dominique Valbelle. *Naissance des cités*, Paris: Nathan, 1990.

Leick, Gwendolyn. *A Dictionary of Ancient Near Eastern Architecture.* London and New York: Routledge, 1988.

Leick, Gwendolyn. *The Invention of the City.* London: Allen Lane, The Penguin Press, 2001.

Liverani, Mario. *L'origine della città. Le prime comunità urbane del Vicino Oriente.* Roma: Editori Riuniti, 1986.

Liverani, Mario. "Power and Citizenship". In Peter Clark (ed.). *The Oxford Handbook of Cities in World History.* Oxford: Oxford University Press, 2013, pp. 164-180.

Liverani, Mario. *Uruk, the First City.* London: Equinox, 2006.

Margueron, Jean-Claude. *Cités invisibles : La naissance de l'urbanisme au Proche-Orient.* Paris: Librairie Orientaliste Paul Geuthner, 2013.

Margueron, Jean-Claude. "L'apparition des villes au Proche-Orient, IVe-IIIe millénaires". In Michel Mazoyer et al. (eds.). *Ville et pouvoir : origines et développements.* Paris: Cahiers Kubaba, Harmattan, 2002, Vol. 1, pp. 216-242.

Margueron, Jean-Claude. "Remarques sur l'organisation de l'espace architectural en Mésopotamie". In *Archéologie de l'Iraq du début du néolithique à 333 avant notre ère.* Paris: Colloques internationaux du CNRS, 580, Paris, 1980, pp. 157-169.

Masetti-Rouault, Maria-Grazia: "Du bon usage de la mythologie mésopotamienne". In X. Faivre, B. Lion and C. Michel (eds), *Et il y eut un esprit dans l'Homme. Jean Bottéro et la Mésopotamie.* Paris: Éditions De Boccard, 2009, pp.19-29.

Michalowski, Piotr. "Divine Heroes and Historical Self-Representation: From Gilgamesh to Shulgi". *Bulletin of the Society of Mesopotamian Studies*, 16, 1988, pp. 19-23.

Michel, Cécile (ed.). *De la maison à la ville dans l'Orient ancien : La ville et les débuts de l'urbanisation.* Nanterre: Cahier des Thèmes transversaux ArScAn, Vol. XI (2011-2012), 2013.

Mieroop, Marc van De. *The Ancient Mesopotamian City.* Oxford: Oxford University Press, 1997.

Olson, Charles. *Collected Prose.* D. Allen, B. Friedlander and R. Creeley (eds.). Berkeley: University of California Press, 1997.

Pezzoli-Olgiati, Daria. *Immagini urbane: Interpretationi religiose della città antica.* Göttingen: Vandenhoeck & Ruprecht, 2002.

Polignac, François de. *Cults, Territory, and the Origins of the Greek City-State.* Chicago: The University of Chicago Press, 1995.

Pournelle, Jennifer R. *Marshland of Cities: Deltaic Landscapes and the Evolution of Early Mesopotamian Civilization.* Dissertation. San Diego: University of California, 2003.

Ragavan Deena (ed.). *Heaven on Earth: Temples, Ritual, and Cosmic Symbolism in the Ancient World.* Chicago: Oriental Institute, 2013.

Stone, Elizabeth C. "The Development of Cities in Mesopotamia". In J. Baines, G. Beckman and K. Rubinson (eds.). *Civilizations of the Ancient Near East.* New York: Charles Scribner's Sons, 1995, Vol. I, pp. 235-248.

Stone, Elizabeth C. "The Spatial Organization of Mesopotamian Cities". *Aula Orientalis*, 9, 1991, pp. 235-242.

Veenhof, Klaas R. (ed.). *Houses and Household in Ancient Mesopotamia.* Leiden: Nederlands Instituut voor het Nabije Oosten/Netherlands Institute for the Near East (NINO), 1996.

Winter, Irene J. "Reading Concepts of Space from Ancient Mesopotamian Monuments". In Kapila Vatsyayan (ed.). *Concepts of Space: Ancient and Modern.* New Delhi: Indira Gandhi National Centre for the Arts, 1991, pp. 55-74.